Ninpô:
Wisdom for Life

NINPÔ

Wisdom for Life

By Masaaki Hatsumi
Grandmaster of Togakure Ryu

Publisher:
Joe Maurantonio (*shidôshi*)

Translators:
Hideaki Tokumitsu, Naoko Yokota
& Joe Maurantonio

Photographs By:
Someya Ken'ichi

Joe Maurantonio (*Editor*)
P. O. Box 146
Yonkers, NY 10710, USA
www.kihon.com

Library of Congress Number 2001099039

ISBN # 0-9727738-0-0

Acknowledgements:
This project could not have been accomplished without the encouraging words of Masaaki Hatsumi. Personal acknowledgements go to Hideaki Tokumitsu, Cathy Blanco, Ben Jones, Glenn Catania, Mark O'Brien, Fred Feddeck, and the Bujinkan New York Dojo.
For Janet, with love.

Note:
The Editor and Translators of this work would like to express their apologies for any inadequacies in this translation. Every effort was made to keep the "flavor" of the original text. Be aware that many social and cultural differences exist from our country to that of the author. If you have any questions please contact Mr. Maurantonio at the address listed above.

CONTENTS

FORWARD TO THIS EDITION

How long ago did I write the book called ***Hiden Togakure Ryu Ninpô***? I almost cannot recall. Surely, it has been more than ten years now. Originally, it was going to be published with the title of ***My Point of View, My Way of Thought***. However, the publishing company decided to publish it with the title of ***Hiden Togakure Ryu Ninpô***.

Back when this book was written, I was spending most of my days training. This is why I feel that this book reflects my youth and the signs of the times. I hope that my younger readers will read this book with the sensitivity of their youth.

Please keep in mind that this book was written while my training was devoted to the lessons of the *kihon happo* [lit. fundamental eight ways] in *taijutsu*. When I looked over this book, the rhythm of "Gone Are the Days" came to mind.

During recent years, the *Bujinkan* has passed from an era of studying *ninjutsu* and grown into the world of *Budô Taijutsu*. Does this cause you to wonder about the direction of the *Bujinkan* in the future?

We are going to advance into the realms of the *happo hiken, ninpô, heihô* and *kenpô*. Furthermore, I would like you all to comprehend the significance of *bufu ikkan*.

Hatsumi Masaaki, *July 1996*

INTRODUCTION

ENLIGHTENMENT DERIVED FROM HIDDEN LIVING

Long ago the *ninja* were known as technicians who exclusively trained for spying and assassination. If a ninja had heard this definition, he would have been angered and replied with a strong response like *bureimono* [insolent fellow]. This prejudiced definition was prevalent because it related back to the popular origin of the ninja perceived as Samurai warriors who had been defeated in war.

The character for *nin* is composed of the Chinese character elements for "sword" [on the top] and "heart" [on the bottom]; this was because a ninja is understood to be an individual who accomplished his aims with cool-hearted behavior that was derived from arduous training. However, the ninja described in the previous paragraph was classified as a subordinate of the clan. The true ninja was a man who had a compassionate heart, and respected and loved peace.

The *nin* for ninja refers to taking care of [or paying attention to] one's own body, mind, and knowledge. The idea concerning one's body and mind is easier to understand, but the idea of taking care of one's knowledge is harder to master. I may have mastered it only quite recently. I understand that it means to pay attention to all one's senses and to your intuition.

The clothes of the ninja were called *ninniku yoroi. Ninniku* is another name for a Buddhist priest's robe. The spirit of the ninja is the essence of *ninniku seishin,* the abandonment of bitterness that results from insults, anger, and jealousy. *Nin* is not placed over the heart in a threatening manner but rather with warm affection, like *kajo waraku* [flower nature, enjoy peace] which has love like a flower and takes pleasure in peace. The way of the ninja is to make his form disappear, to naturally escape from the enemy's sword, and to overcome the enemy using the natural powers of *chi, sui, ka, fu, ku,* [earth, water, fire, wind, and sky] to protect his nation and people.

Above, I noted the belief that the ninja's origins were a result of lost battles, but they did not persevere simply because they wanted to save their own lives. Rather, they endured the shame and struggles of their loss [lost battles] and survived in order to see to the fate of their lords and protect their own nation. Consequently, they developed their own philosophy of *bugei* [warriorship].

Many years ago, ninja stories and fables were very popular. Many movies, television programs, and novels were created in which ninja were depicted as heartless people, but this is far from the truth. These movie ninja pursued their own goals even when the result was a miserable death. These mistakes were made because the authors or writers did not have enough knowledge about the ninja. Even more shocking, was that these authors wrote their theories upon the ninja and arrogantly pretended as if they themselves had mastered *ninjutsu* and become true ninja. That situation not only made me angry but also looked so strange and humorous to us [those of us training]. How many of those writers and authors discerned that one has to study at least eight areas of knowledge to become a ninja?

The *ninja hachimon* [eight gates of the ninja] refers to *kiai*, *koppo taijutsu*, *kenjutsu*, *sojutsu*, *shuriken*, *kajutsu*, *yugei*, and *kyumon*. Whatever one's tradition or school minimally, these basic eight subjects were required to become a ninja. Those who mastered more than these eight subjects were truly called ninja. In *Togakure ryu,* we learn eighteen subjects which are Spiritual Refinement, *koppo taijutsu*, *kenpô*, *bôjutsu*, *shuriken*, *kusarigama*, *yari*, *naginata*, *kisha jutsu*, *suiren*, *kayaku jutsu*, *boryaku*, *choho*, *shinobi aruki*, *inton*, *henso jutsu*, *tenmon* and *chimon*. Then *kyojitsu tenkan ho* [exchanging truth and falsehood] was added onto these subjects and they became the basic structure of *Togakure ryu ninjutsu*. This *kyojitsu tenkan ho* is the most secret technique in all *budô*.

Once when I gave a lecture, I was asked this question: "Having heard your lecture, a ninja appears to be a gentleman. If so, then why did they sneak into people's houses and steal things?" I answered, "As the Buddha said, 'it is sometimes duplicity that makes things improve.' A ninja who understood the way of men truly used cunning to protect their nation and their people."

A ninja often appeared to be the least skilled person in any field, as is shown in many movies and novels. A ninja who was poor and of lower social status was assumed to be antisocial. It has been said that the ninja was a person who never worried about the possibility of death in the pursuit of a better world. A ninja was not such a terrible person [as in the movies]. The ninja were astonishing people who kept trying to persevere even through the worst and most painful circumstances.

Recently, a book concerning the "intellect" became a best-seller. People living in our modern age seem unsatisfied and are preoccupied only with having such an intellect [as described in the book]. I think today is the age for "perspective and endurance." In these difficult modern times, I feel that it is quite important to have a mind and a body for persistence. Finally, I have made my decision to write a book upon the ninja who endure through difficult times and on the relationship between ninja and modern dilemmas.

Of course, this book may not be pragmatic for everyone, on the other hand, if it helps anyone to spend his or her daily life better, I will be very pleased.

Masaaki Hatsumi

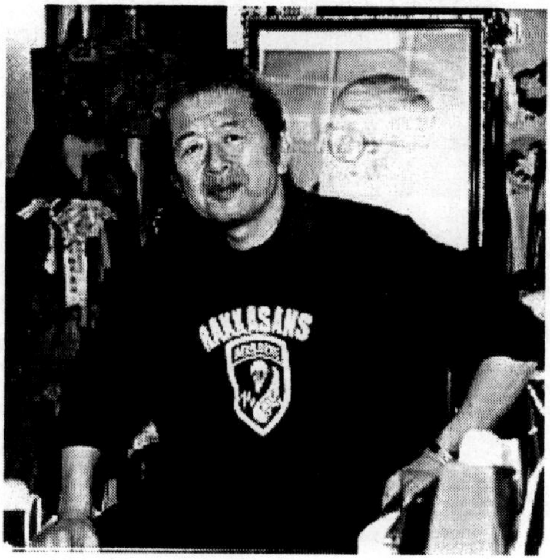

CHAPTER ONE

PHILOSOPHY OF BUDÔ AND NINPÔ

This chapter contains the basic theme of this book. Therefore, I would like you to read it over and over to appreciate it.

PHILOSOPHY OF BUDÔ

In a broad sense *bujutsu* means to protect one's country and to a narrower extent, it means to protect your community, your family and yourself. *Bujutsu* is not only a technique with a sword, but also a technique with your mind. To learn how to strike is *kenjutsu*, to learn how to chop is chopping wood. [Techniques without conscious awareness are bland and rhythmical].

While *jutsu* means technique and must contain *waza* [skills], *jutsu* must also have heart. If your heart is not pure, your technique will not be reliable. If you have a good heart, your technique will be good. Purpose is the same as *jutsu* and if there is no purpose, there is no *jutsu*. True victory relies not upon you, but on your enemy. Thus, victory comes naturally to you. You have only to wait for it to happen. Do not search for victory or seek gain, allow it to happen naturally: just as flint and steel come together naturally to make fire.

Even if you are an eighth *dan* (or a master), there is no evidence that you are good. You have to deeply taste a beautiful technique. If you think it exists, it does not. If you think it does not, it does. When you and your sword come together, that is the foundation of *bu* [the Martial path].

PHILOSOPHY OF NINJUTSU

The essence of martial arts is self-defense. However, the essence of self-protection lies in *ninjutsu* because *ninjutsu* also protects one's spirit. Without the proper spirit in martial training, one can be lead to ruin.

For example, medical technology is dedicated to healing lives, but when misused it can also harm people. Food and drink are necessary for nourishment. However, overeating harms the body. Politicians are responsible for governing countries and protecting the interests of the people, but when these individuals become greedy, ignorant and are afraid to commit their lives to their endeavors, they only bring about disorder and cause suffering. A religion, when it is sincere and steadfast, can inspire people to protect themselves, make their families thrive, and benefit society. When corrupt, it destroys people and puts the nation in jeopardy.

If you are a martial artist and master *budô* and practice *ninjutsu*, you will gain the most essential secret of all methods. This secret is called the *shin-shin shin-gan,* "mind and eyes of god." This knowledge is to know *Tendô*, "the path of heaven." The truth of heaven is the correct way, without evil intent.

People must have faith. This is the only justice that exists in heaven and in society. Wood, fire, soil, metal, water and spring, summer, fall, winter cannot exist without the Earth. The four seasons and the five elemental manifestations balance the Earth in the same manner as truth balances heaven.

If a person is honest, virtuous and faithful, he is walking upon "the path of heaven." When he goes with the path of heaven, he is following the will of heaven. This is the "mind and eyes of god." Therefore, a ninja has to be a sensible and righteous person. Ninjutsu methods of perseverance can also be understood as methods of perception. A ninja is always calm and never surprised by any situation. This is the *Togakure ryu* martial way.

KEY POINTS TO FINDING THE GOKUI

In the past eras, everyone wanted to get hold of the secret scrolls. It was believed that if you received a scroll you would improve [in training and skill]. Nevertheless, you were to train until the time when you were of ability to receive the secret scroll. Finally, having received it, you become too tense to move. In other words, when you received the scroll, you should not do any technique wrong. Then, after several years of training, you would become capable of handling the weight [burden] of it. That is the first time when you would be in true possession of the scroll because you would know [feel] the belief and preparedness [resolution] of having the secret scrolls deeply in your heart.

When people train in karate, they sometimes wear iron *geta* [traditional Japanese platform sandals]. At first, these *geta* feel heavy, but eventually the wearer gets used to them. Receiving the scroll is like this idea. It is heavy at first but eventually it gets lighter.

What are the *gokui* [essential teachings]? My teacher, Takamatsu *sensei*, used to be nicknamed "Mongolian Tiger." In China, he was a young warrior feared by many. However, in Japan, a friend visited him and said Takamatsu (who lived in Yamato) was more like a "Yamato house cat." Takamatsu responded, "Since I have become a house cat, I can live longer and women like to cuddle me."

Someone once asked me, "Hatsumi *sensei*, why don't you fight with a bull?" I replied, "A bull is much stronger than I am, therefore, I would lose. Nevertheless, a farmer can put a ring in a bull's nose and lead the bull anywhere he wants it to go. I would do the same. Why couldn't a ninja put a ring through a bull's nose, too?"

A secret teaching is an insight and preparedness of a person. In other words, if you want to get the secret teachings you must always be prepared to answer the types of questions like those Takamatsu and I have answered. In this sense, everybody has the nature [gift] to understand the secret teachings and to teach them to their students.

Because the ninja could climb walls and hang upside down, they could view [perceive] things differently. The world can often be a bad place and you must sometimes look at things from a different perspective in order to see society's good points.

According to the *denshô* [written transmissions], *yari*, *bô*, and *ken* [sword] techniques should be natural, flowing body movements. These should be done without thinking about the technique. From nothing [not thinking], something [an action] comes forth, and the person who masters this idea is the one who can comprehend the secret teachings. This understanding in your heart is more important than the techniques. The mind of "*munen muso*" [no thought, no mind] in the heart is the real secret teaching rather than the *waza* [skills].

ENDURING THE KNOWLEDGE

There is a trend that people who are good at social discourse become popular and will often rise to the top of their respective businesses. Those who are clumsy and ordinary will most likely not rise to the top. Students sometimes complain that people who do not have enough knowledge often get promoted to the top.

In such a case, I answer like this, "When I was young, I would often fight with foolish people. I was a real brat. I was poor at socializing, too. As I grew older, my rhythm (timing) in dealing with people got better. What is important is not to forget your purpose and goal. As I told you before, if you become a raccoon you can trick other people [in Japan, a raccoon is thought to have powers that can deceive people] but you do not trick yourself. For warrior arts, you must gain knowledge, but on the other hand, it is also important to endure knowledge. In simpler terms, to endure the knowledge is to know the time when you should use the knowledge and when you should not use it. You must become a person who can do this."

The student said, "So, that is why you socialize with some people who are not so prominent. You sometimes act so wild and spontaneous that it makes us nervous. But now we understand you were socializing with them within that context." The other students nodded in agreement.

Even if a person is stubborn and lacks knowledge, if you can match your rhythm with his, sometimes you can still find him a very nice person. When you are young, you feel that people who have no knowledge are stupid and you get sick of them, but at that time, you should have the perseverance to go forth and deal with those people. Those who have this type of perseverance are truly brave people.

If you promote valor, and can match rhythm, you should encourage our young people, our next generation, to go forth with knowledge and understanding and clean our environment. I believe that from now on people should improve [current environmental problems] by asserting their knowledge and intelligence.

DO NOT NEGLECT SELF-TRAINING

Modern *budô* students often forget to practice by themselves. I used to practice by myself. When there was no teacher, I found the secret teachings by my own desire. I used to go into the mountains and train with nature (trees, animals, etc.). I used to do *uchikomi* [striking skills], *sakanage* [throwing reversals], *nagewaza* [throwing techniques], *sabaki* [evading techniques], *moguri* [diving] and *taihenjutsu* [ground hitting skills] with trees. Similarly, I would train with animals. I would often read their intention, evade them, and practice *nagewaza* with the bigger animals. I learned to predict and to use the changes of nature. I did *sumo* with nature, also. In this way, I trained myself for my own benefit.

Of course, it would be better to have a teacher. However, if the teacher were bad, you would only learn the movements and not the true essence of the martial arts. Recently, a book called ***Honin Shugi*** [about not interfering with a person's development] became a best-seller and we should be satisfied with it. This approach shows people can become creative sometimes.

Some students find it difficult to learn regardless how hard you teach them. Nevertheless, some truly have a passion for *budô*. I leave these students alone, do not say anything to them, nor provide them with explanations. Even if I do this, the student who really loves *budô* will come every day, practice and still gain something like "*moanzen no kozo*." No matter what the problem is, I believe that too much teaching is not desirable.

Mr. Oyomei had a technique called *do-in jutsu* and with this technique, he could predict the arrival of people who would be coming to visit. However, he noticed that teaching others this technique was not good for them. Therefore, he stopped teaching them.

Anyway, too much of something is not good. It is the same with *budô*. I have a policy, I do not teach high level techniques to beginners unless they are marvelous students. I believe secret teachings should only be given to those students who can find and create new lessons for themselves. This is because the secret teachings are not about how many techniques one knows, but rather about a person's insight and preparedness.

The non-interference policy is a method of education that was born from spiritual awakening of "nothingness." No human being should be brought up with the sense of modern education in which everything comes from something [already present].

Often I tell high school students, "It seems young people study reluctantly. This is because you do not have any determination or intent in your life. Now I am going to teach you. First, try to fall in love with one thing. Fall in love with *ninpô*. This is within your grasp. To fall in love with one thing is to give birth to a thousand possibilities. I hope you will understand since you are almost adults. If you fall in love with *ninpô*, you can practice all by yourself. Then from there you will learn many things."

Because people from all over the world come to see me, I began to study many languages. You must study, even to learn a single thing, no matter if it is the history of *budô*, ideas, religion, philosophy, language, psychology, chemistry, physics, etc. You learn to study by yourself. It is more important to learn by yourself instead of being taught techniques by a teacher. I often remind my students, and myself, "Life is to practice by myself." This is my guide to life. In addition, if you do train with others it is important to pay attention to them.

DEVOTE YOURSELF TO TRAINING

To master one *waza* is not only valuable for people studying *budô*, but for anyone who studies anything. A doctor once told me, "The brain weighs between 1300 - 1500 grams. Scientists say that the heavier your brain is the smarter you are. And strange to say, if you weighed the brain of a talented person who had fully mastered one skill or ability, it would probably weigh about 1500 grams." This leads me to believe that it is important to train every day to master an art.

The men in the *Kabuki* [Japanese drama] theaters who play women are supposed to spend their daily lives as women [to perfect their art]. What is the most important ability for those who study the martial arts? It is, of course, to learn not to give up. To improve in my martial training, I trained three times as hard [as my peers] in mental training, three times as hard in physical training and I spent three times as much money to become strong. When I became strong, I found myself being weak in other places. I tried to figure out why I was weak but I could not. Although I became confused, I trained myself believing, without any hesitation, that if I accomplished one new skill or ability I would be spiritually enlightened. One day I became ill and was unable to overcome my confusion. My heartbeat became very fast as if it was telling me the danger of my ways. I was even unable to stand. During the five years that followed, I believed death was perhaps easier than life. Before this time, I was proud of my power. Yet, in truth, I was not as strong as I thought and so I felt as though I had been defeated.

Even through all of this, I never was absent from my training. I recovered naturally. Then, I thought that getting old, getting sick, and dying, was all a part of training. When you are fine, you should practice as though you are fine, if you are old, you should practice as though you are old, and when you are dying, you should practice "beyond life and death." I have learned this was the correct way to approach training. Being sick for five years made me forget what was strong and what was weak. I learned natural techniques that did not rely upon physical power. I also learned that if I had a hard time training, I could train with others and make them happy.

During my training, I would sometimes get really sick and tired of my own stupidity [of being unable to do a technique]. There is a time when people get into a slump, like when their *waza* are not done correctly, they cannot practice it like it is supposed to be done, and their opponent keeps beating them. I believe this period is like a snake shedding its skin and I regard it as a time to grow better. The accumulation of each shed skin is the proof of our growth and promotion in *dan* (level). When you are having a difficult time, other people's techniques always seem very good. It is like a child thinking another child's toy is better than his own. If your bad period lasts for ten years, you should consider stopping *budô*.

It is important to know the basis of *budô* when you start practicing. Those who study *budô* should not concentrate solely upon the techniques. If you wholeheartedly devote yourself to technique-oriented *budô*, you will only be a *budô* researcher.

I have met many martial artists who understood how to do techniques but did not understand the essence of *budô*. They were only intoxicated with the martial arts as a decoration and decorated their conversation with it. This way of thinking is just "flowers" [i.e., decoration] and these people have forgotten the foundations of the martial arts. If someone keeps on training without knowing the foundation and how it "blooms into a flower," then it is certain he will have a "hollow mind and eyes." In *budô* training you must first have a root [foundation] and then this will grow [develop] into a big tree [greater ability]. In this way, a seed grows and a flower blooms.

When I am training intensely, I will sometimes have a weird dream. This is a story about my teacher, Toshitsugu Takamatsu, who really enjoyed drawing and painting. He would draw from 5:00 a.m. to noon every day. One day, he painted a picture of a dragon for his friend. A few nights later, my teacher dreamed about a dragon that had no eyes. The dragon said to him, "I want eyes." The next morning he called his friend and his friend told him in the painting the dragon had no eyes.

The training of *budô* is the same, if you train every day, you will sometimes dream about the techniques you had a hard time mastering. Therefore, the secret teachings of *budô* are introduced as "dreams from the gods." Miyamoto Musashi often wrote about his dreams. If you are intent about something, you will slowly come to an understanding of it. Therefore, those who are not determined cannot gain secret teachings, even if they have access to secret teachings. Some people think they must have talent to join training, but talent comes to you depending on how often you train. You should try training harder rather than looking for where your talent lies.

What is the purpose of those who train in *budô*? Your purpose is the most important thing when training. Some people may train in *budô* because they want to be strong, or to make them feel more at ease about entering a higher grade in school, or to get better jobs, or to become an instructor and make a lot of money or to feel superior. Maybe I should say this is okay because everyone has their own purpose, but in the old days, those who were called *bujin* or *kensei* [sword saints] did not have such purposes. They mastered *budô* for their own training. They believed training was good for other people too, instead of only for themselves. You should stop training that is not beneficial to yourself and others.

Training greatly effects the molding of character. By making it a custom to train correctly, a person can change his personality and integrity.

I hope every one of you becomes a person who can see their lives illuminated by the light of training. Consequently, know that the most dangerous way of thinking is to pretend you know everything. If you do not know something, it is okay. It is important to know that you do not know.

SOMETHING WILL BE BORN OF ENTHUSIASM

You must train enthusiastically. When you lose enthusiasm, training becomes a problem. If you lose your enthusiasm before you are proficient at *budô*, your techniques will become useless [lifeless]. It is the same with iron and pottery. Heat has a lot to do with enthusiasm, excitement, devotion, and passion. Anyway, you need this "heat" to produce things and to make changes. Fire yourself with enthusiasm, keep control of bad and evil, follow a righteous path, this is the essence of training. From here, spiritual awakening is born. The spiritual awakening in *budô* is called the "secret of *budô*." The "secret of *budô*" [*gokui*] was often very difficult to understand when it was written in the *makimono* [scrolls]. Japanese people often make things seem more formidable than they are. Actually, the "secret of *budô*" is not very difficult.

Gokui is just like an equation in mathematics. The circumference of a circle is 3.14159...[π or pi]. This is the *gokui* of a circle. If you say it like this, the concept of π [pi] may seem very simple, but you would never know how much effort was put into the discovery of that equation. Many of these types of concepts make one big *gokui*. Just like my Israeli student said, "Japanese *budô* has no end to it." In the *denshô*, techniques are divided into four levels: *shoden*, *chuden*, *okuden*, and *kaiden*. Those who have never studied or have only studied a little of the martial arts often ask me how many techniques I know. I say I have never counted them and they are surprised because they think there are too many to count. While there are many techniques in the *shoden*, *chuden*, *okuden*, and *kaiden* I do not waste my time dividing and numbering them.

For those who research *budô*, the number of techniques is important, but for those of us, who train in *budô*, the number is not important. The harmony of *bu* is what is important. If you do not consider the harmony of *bu* to be important, your techniques will be like those of a beginner even if you know all the techniques in the *shoden*, *chuden*, *okuden*, and *kaiden*.

MUSHA SHUGYO

It is said the phrase *musha shugyo* [warrior errantry] came into usage at the end of the *Ashikaga* era [circa 1573]. At first, *musha shugyo* suggested a *ronin* [masterless Samurai] who was working as a temporary retainer. Later, the term came to signify traveling around the country to train in *budô* and develop into a better warrior. There were different types of *musha shugyo*. Some warriors did *musha shugyo* by challenging other fighters to combat, some warriors did *musha shugyo* by working for the feudal government, and others remained jobless and traveled about the country. The choice, of course, depended upon the individual and the era in which they lived.

Many people want to know if warriors needed *musha shugyo* and how one should go about doing it. Your opinion of *musha shugyo* [on it being necessary or not] lies mainly in your motivations. In times past, some warriors had decided to go out and find a good teacher, others wanted to determine their ability as a warrior, many wanted to evaluate their techniques, and others decided to go on self-imposed quests. For these people, *musha shugyo* was to go beyond the bounds of simple training. You must stretch beyond your personal limitations.

Recently, many people have had a chance to go overseas, and they boast about it. Those who have not had the same chance often feel inferior. I feel bad for those people who went abroad just to drink and look at women and not to explore culture and see good sights. I think it is important to have a good attitude and purpose when traveling. For example, famous paintings of naked women are just pornography to those people who do not know the worth of true paintings. Anyway, it is important to see various countries. Martial artists should meet and talk with fellow martial artists all over the world.

Fortunately, martial artists from all over the world visit me and I am lucky enough to do my *musha shugyo* at my home. Nevertheless, someday I would like to go to some foreign countries to see their martial arts.

I often hear stories about fighting in other countries. I have heard of the true story of Mr. Koyama, who went to China during the Second World War. "I was in charge of a unit and in that unit there was a man who was a black belt. The black belt fought using judo with a Chinese *Kung Fu* artist and lost. Japanese black belts and Chinese martial artists would sometimes fight in *kendô* and *bujutsu*. Though the Japanese wore protective gear and the Chinese did not wear any protective armor, they could not get near the Chinese. These contests usually came to a draw. Maybe, because the Chinese had weak backs the Japanese won at *sumo*. At any rate, the Chinese were much better at gambling. I realized the big difference was,

Japanese believe that class distinctions are important, while the Chinese people believe that protecting themselves was most important." By watching the boys at the martial arts' schools in China you can see this is true.

My teacher, Toshitsugu Takamatsu, had experienced a number of challenge matches and if he was in thirty matches, he won all of these. Takamatsu once had a match with a man named Choshiryu, who was a *kung fu* master. Choshiryu was a student of Chosarin. This match became one of the big talks of Shin Province. Choshiryu was a very large and broad-shouldered man. One day, Choshiryu went to Takamatsu and challenged him to a match. However, Takamatsu refused twice because he said the real *budô* of Japan was not fighting. The third time when Choshiryu challenged, Takamatsu accepted believing it would be an insult to *bumon* if he refused again. The fighting place was packed. There were a great many people outside who had come to watch. It was too crowded to even fight there so they had to move to the open space of Sokai nearby, and then fight. Choshiryu was about twice as large as Takamatsu. Takamatsu constantly avoided Choshiryu's attacks. This went on for more than an hour until Choshiryu was perspiring like a demon and was exhausted. Takamatsu tried to attack him, but the referee yelled, "*Sore madé,*" [it's time]. The match was over. After the fight, the two men went to eat at a nearby restaurant.

At that time, Choshiryu admitted, "I have had many matches, but I have never had as good a fight as this before. If the referee had not called time, I would have lost for sure." Takamatsu said, "No, you could have fought a lot longer." Choshiryu replied, "Thank you for your words. Indeed, Takamatsu, you are strong. Please, be my *buyu* [martial brother]." They talked, they drank, and they became like brothers. In time, Choshiryu was unfortunately killed in a bombing attack.

It is good to learn both *uchi* [inner] and *soto* [outer] realities of a situation, not only in *budô,* but also in the rest of life, as well. If you can train in *budô* when you are young, you can do a great deal for society when you grow up. So then, *musha shugyo* is useful for learning about society and, most important, for developing an understanding of ourselves.

TO BECOME A STUDENT

A teacher is essential not only for warriors, but for those who wish to learn almost anything. Having an exceptional teacher and training diligently allows you to become an exemplary warrior, but it is almost impossible for you to learn true *budô* if your teacher is only doing his teaching as an occupation.

In the old days, when someone wanted to become a student, he had to search for a teacher, or maybe, a teacher would find him in the mountains while he was there doing some training. In either case, the teacher would decide whether the prospective student was worth training or not. Those who wanted to be students often had to cut firewood and clean rooms for their teachers. This went on for years and years, cutting wood and cleaning rooms from morning to night. During those years, the teacher would determine if the student were worth training by how much focus and determination the student had to persevere and learn *budô*. Then, when the proper moment arose, the teacher would say, "Come to the *dojo*. I will give you some training." During the arduous daily training, the student would then become a genuine student and would begin to realize the blessings of his teacher and how much his teacher must have cared for him.

Nowadays, people who wish to become my students come to see me for a variety of reasons; some are frail and cowardly so they desire to become strong, some are intellectuals and wish to make their spirit strong, and some just want to be strong in fighting ability. Their reasons vary, but they all say they want to learn and *seem* to have a longing for *budô*.

I tell these people honestly, "If you want to forge your spirit, then just believe in religion. *Budô* means learning the best techniques with which to kill people. If you want to make your body stronger, then go for walks, lift weights, and eat plenty of vegetables. What good would be accomplished by becoming strong in *budô*? In true *budô*, you can't win any trophies or make your riches."

While saying these things, I watch their reactions. Although I let some become my students, few can persist in the training. Few people are *fools* enough to continue their training and hold onto their determination regardless of what others say about them. Takamatsu *sensei* once allowed one *fool* [Hatsumi *sensei*] to become his student after reading him this poem:

In the first year of the Tenei era
there was a great master of Koppo.
He lived calmly and peacefully
like flowers in the Spring.
But he was so courageous that he was
never afraid of fighting against
one hundred thousand enemies.
He could strike down a wild animal
with but a single blow.

This is not boasting nor am I telling an untruth. A person who cannot become a *fool* will fail in all their actions... These people live lives that lead to misery because they only pursue everything halfheartedly. I am fortunate to have a few students whom I know are true *fools*.

Now, between a teacher and student there must be a proper feeling of respect. Takamatsu *sensei* used to address me as "Hatsumi *sensei*" and this was always a little embarrassing. It was hard for me to comprehend why he would address me in this fashion. Now I realize that there was proper respect between us, and again I would like to bow to his wisdom.

However, a teacher is a teacher and a student is a student. Do not forget to thank your teacher and be respectful. I found my purpose in life and my passion because of Takamatsu *sensei*. There is a Japanese phrase, which holds an abundance of truth: "Parents and child are one generation; husband and wife are the second; yet the student and teacher relationship is third."

RELIGION, FAITH & BUDÔ

In 500 B.C., according to historical records, people who believed in Buddhism came to Japan to attack the government. The government tried to defend itself with *bô,* bows and arrows, and other weapons. They also built fortifications around important regions to protect their country. This is the oldest record of Japanese warfare. You could call it a religious war. Just through a slight corruption, religion and beliefs can become powerful weapons.

Those who train in *budô* must be discriminating about religious study. In the past, it seems that many wars were simply about religious differences. Today, most of our wars seem to be about differing beliefs. This is why we all need to know the proper principles of religion and faith. If you do not know this, you will be fighting forever, just because of the differences in religion or belief.

In 1972, the Japanese Red Army killed many of its own members. Some of the people who were arrested became remorseful and began to wonder why they had done such things. This shows how people can forget human virtue simply by becoming intoxicated with religion and philosophy. Without proper restraint, some intoxicated people can become murderers.

> The Buddha tried to reach nirvana, or the awakening of spiritual oneness, through the spiritual practice he developed. In Brahminism, people tried to reach universal god by faith and austere discipline, and find fortune through the power of the Creator.
>
> In Christianity, people seek the essence of God as mercy; they try to appease sin and to gain goodness and a stable life. Japanese Shinto tries to balance the spirit by sweeping away "mental inertia" and impurity, by calming the soul, and by teaching how to acquire a peaceful life.
>
> Four Japanese Buddhist monks in Yoshinoyama Sozanji (Shinei, Dozen, Shogo, and Gomyo) started the practice of scholasticism followed by Dengyo and Kobo Daishi [famous monks] by combining Shintoism and Buddhism and taught the peaceful life. Tenrikyo ["Divine Wisdom"] taught the principle of fate and the law of cause-and-effect, or reward according to a deed, and viewed it as life's destiny.

> The principle of *Seicho no Ie* ["Truth of Life"] involves trying to understand the human spirit in a philosophical way called *shinsokan* [prayerful meditation], regarding the spirit as primary, and trying to find peace of mind. The principles of *Daigen-kyo*, *Hito no dokyo*, and *konko-kyo* are based on soul-calming faith, diminishing the pain of life, and acquiring peace of mind.

There are many other religions and denominations, but all of them have the analogous belief of protecting their heart. Religion is necessary to keep peace no matter where we live. Religion was originally a teaching of nature and is important that it fit into the society of its time. To believe in something is to move toward what you believe in. Yet, you should not rely upon religion, no matter how much you donate to the church. If your behavior is not ethical then you cannot gain anything. It is important to understand the virtue of air, earth, and heaven, and understand the purpose of believing in religion.

STRIVE TO KNOW YOUR RANK

If you consider the *sôke* [head of the family] of a tradition [*ryu*] as a river then *dan* [black belt levels] are comparable to river life. Tenth *dan* is one of the highest ranks. Rank is an honor to those who train as well as a source of inspiration. It is fine for it to be considered in this way, but *dan* is more like a reward for a warrior, a medal for a military person or a family crest for a man. In this light, rank is something in which you can take pride.

If society becomes corrupt, then *budô* will also become corrupt. Furthermore, those without true ability begin to be promoted by way of trickery or deception.

The less ability you have the more famous you want to become. A person with no ability but who becomes famous would always need to keep people with genuine ability away. This type of person would gather the people with no ability, and thus diminish the pathways of the martial arts. The *sôke* of a tradition must not succumb to this way of thought, but rather must deny those who have no sincere potential.

Whenever I give rank to my students, I say, "I am the one who gave you this *dan*, but it is you who must keep its worth." Rank is given to keep harmony among students training in the martial arts. People with higher *dan* guide those who have lower *dan* and those who have lower *dan* show respect to those who have higher *dan*. In order to do this, higher rank people must sometimes scold people of lower rank, but this is only an expression of their devotion. This leads to harmony and cooperation. Likewise, this means to love and protect your country. Knowing your skill level is the best way to value your ranking. If you have a *shodan* train as a *shodan* and, in this fashion, it will lead you to *nidan*.

If you are a worker, whatever your job is, whatever your rank might be, you must do your best. Those who do their best can be promoted. For those who complain about their job and do not do their best, though they may be promoted, their seniority has little or no meaning. According to my experience, the worst thing to be is too conscious of your rank. To show off your *dan* is just like a deranged person abusing a weapon. People who are not too conscious of their rank and train often are truly marvelous.

Recently, the number of foreigners who come to Japan to train has increased. There are two types of these visitors: those who are looking for rank and those who are looking for instruction. They think that to be a *dan*, which is awarded from a Japanese person is just great for business. Many think that *budô* is all about money. I have instructed all in the same manor, regardless of where they come from. Perhaps, this was wrong of me.

You must start *budô* with clear intent; you must throw away your confusion. If a human being becomes zero, the numbers from one to nine are born, and there is the accessibility to gain *kuji*, *juji*, or *myojutsu*. However, only those who are devoted to *budô* can understand this truly. It is often difficult for foreigners to comprehend these ideas. When a foreign student asked me for rank because he wanted to return to Holland and be a police instructor, I told him, "I will make you a *godan* for *bujutsu*. Of course, I expect you to be an exemplary practitioner of *budô* and will give you this license for your happiness. This is the value of *dan* in the martial arts." This foreign student kept saying how he was very happy. I could see how happy it had made him and I thought this *dan* is much more valuable than the *dan* that simply displays who is stronger or weaker.

Let me discuss how a teacher used to give rank to his students. This understanding is imperative for us to converse about *dan* in the clan. Matsumoto Bizen Nakami [founder of the *Kashima Shin ryu*] divided his essential teachings [*gokui*] into three parts, which were *ichi no ten*, *ni no tachi*, and *sanshigoku*. *Ichi no ten*, also called *kurai dori*, used knowledge of the change in climate or weather to obtain a dominant position. *Ni no tachi* is using nature to have a dominant position. *Sanshigoku* is courage rather than techniques: no doubt, no confusion, and no fear. These three are the unification of *seishin ryoku* [mental or spiritual powers]. Of course, it was necessary to have technique and *kata* also, but it was much more important to have morals, ethics, and philosophy as a person who trains in *budô*. With this in mind, you can understand why you would be defeated if you only trained in technique.

I think the phrases "*itto nanpo*" [if you wish to use a sword you must have much experience] and "*isshi nanpo*" [you must have a broad moral and philosophical base] were born from a combination of techniques, morals, and philosophy. Knowing many ways of using a sword was not enough to get *dan* ranking. The important factors in the secret teachings [*hiden*] were the students' preparedness and the students' mental attitude. The clan gives *dan* to these students.

A VIEW OF BUDÔ FROM "BLUE EYES"

Japan can be very proud of its established *budô*. However, if you are vain in this regard, you will lose the essential intention of *budô*. Once, I had a chance to speak about the various martial arts with two foreign martial artists. The following is an outline of our discussion:

Hatsumi: What do you think about the Japanese *dan* ranking system?

Foreigner: Japanese *budô* has a *dan* system that I consider a mistake.

Sometimes students can simply purchase a black belt. This can decrease the value of *budô* and make it into a business... simple money making. It may destroy the *seishin* [spirit, intention, etc.] of true *budô*.

Hatsumi: Is this so? It is my belief that since judo became a worldwide sport; judo practitioners should not be ranked and should simply concentrate on the weight-class championships.

Foreigner: In Chinese Shorinji *kenpô*, it takes ten years to go up one level. It then takes forty years to go up four steps and become an instructor.

Hatsumi: The phrase, "one stands in one's forties" may have an origin in such traditions. Japanese people tend to like being called "*sensei*." Everyone can become a teacher instantly. You were traveling around the world and training in different *budô* arts, what is your purpose?

Foreigner: I have two purposes. One is to learn unique techniques of the domestic martial arts in different countries. My other purpose is hoplology, which is the study of combative behavior. When I travel to foreign countries and show my techniques to the martial artists, it often pleases them to show their techniques to me.

Hatsumi: Did sharing techniques with each other form friendships?

Foreigner: Yes. However, in some of the friendly matches fought, many participants became so serious that they forgot about friendship and the interactions became dangerous.

Hatsumi: It is good to know the temperament of people before you start a friendly match.

Foreigner: Later, I often took photographs of their weapons and their techniques. Then I would research the relationship between the different martial arts. For instance, the relationship between Indian and Indonesian martial arts in terms of weaponry and techniques.

Hatsumi: An exceptional idea! I think it is necessary to study a martial art through folk traditions, cultural climate, weapons, and techniques. This is something that I have been doing. However, in Japanese *budô* my perspective is a bit narrow. Japanese martial artists need to know more about other martial arts in the world.

Foreigner: My focus is the study of the people and their weaponry: anthropology and psephology [scientific study of elections].

Hatsumi: What are your thoughts on *seishin* [spirit]?

Foreigner: The *seishin* of a particular man may be great while another may be bad.

Hatsumi: If the *budô seishin* of someone were too narrow-minded, they would appear to be mentally unsound.

Foreigner: Yes. People that do not pass judgement upon others often have stronger vitality in *budô*. When I visited Java [Indonesia], I saw a teacher who after seeing his friend's head was bleeding, touched it with his hands and stopped the blood flow.

Hatsumi: This is a mental ability. On the other hand, perhaps the teacher stimulated an autonomic nerve.

Foreigner: One martial art instructor in Jakarta told me that he could beat an enemy without even touching him. When I asked him if this was true, he answered that he would not do it at that time and showed me a photograph. This was probably a fabrication.

Hatsumi: How did you feel when you visited some of these different countries and saw excellent techniques?

Foreigner: When I saw an excellent technique, I wanted to use it myself. Then I wanted to master it.

Hatsumi: Some techniques are superficial rather than one with many levels and genuine depth. How could you tell the difference between those two?

Foreigner: I used to learn the technique and practice it. If it was a true technique, I could improve with it. However, if it were a sham, I would get bored with it.

Hatsumi: Many traditional martial arts have remained active in their native countries. In most countries, a martial art usually started from primitive fighting methods. In Japan, fight skills developed into *daken taijutsu* and then advanced into *dakenjutsu* and *kakuriki*. Then *dakenjutsu* and *taijutsu* were combined into *daken taijutsu*. Various martial arts such as *jutaijutsu*, jujutsu, *kenpô*, judo, Aikido, and karate in Okinawa were founded based upon *daken taijutsu*.

Foreigner: From very long ago, wrestling existed in Europe and Sumo in Mongolia. There is also an ancient martial art in Egypt. All of these are primitive ones.

Hatsumi: Have you notice the kicks in *Tai Chi Chuan* or *Pa Qua*? It is easy to see that Chinese martial arts are good at kicking forms. Many children play "*hanetsuki*" [battledore and shuttlecock] and this helps to make their legs supple and strong.

Foreigner: Have you heard of the South American martial art that existed around the Amazon River? Its movements look like a wild dance. It is called *Capoiera*. They start from a form like a dance and kick using both legs. The kicks are very effective. Many of the practitioners are very tall and have long legs. Therefore, they kick in elegant forms.

Hatsumi: Do you know that there are many ways to strengthen your fists? The fingernails of Toshitsugu Takamatsu, my *sensei*, were very thick, and he had to maintain them with a file. In my *ryuha*, we use vegetable oils to strengthen one's fist. We do not try to make the hard part of the fist harder, but try to strengthen the soft and frail portion very gradually over a long period.

Foreigner: Some people believe that strengthening a fist takes only a year. However, a year is not long enough. In certain countries, one puts some medicine on the front and side of one's fist and strengthens it throughout one's life. They even did this to their legs, so it strengthens the areas around the bone. If they used that area to kick you, it would be a painful blow. Your hands could easily be broken. In another country, people open, fold, and unfold a piece of paper with a single hand to build up their dexterity. If you continued this every day, your palms would be better for grasping. Your enemy would feel your grasps as quite painful.

Hatsumi: In Japanese Shorinji *kenpô*, practitioners do not study weapons very much. Takamatsu *sensei* told me that even in karate it is better to use a *bô* to fight rather than to fight empty handed. Therefore, I made *bôjutsu* a requirement in my *dojo*.

Foreigner: I have visited Shorin. They had many weapons there and originally in Shorinji *kenpô* they were taught many different weapons. Obviously, fighting with a weapon offers quite an advantage over being unarmed.

Hatsumi: For many centuries, people who think pragmatically have held political influence. Nobunaga came into power by using firearms. Hideyoshi had contests between people with long spears and those with short spears, and those with the long spears won. Western people are known to have a rational way of thinking. What do you think about rationality?

Foreigner: A warrior who carried a sword with him seemed brave compared to a person with a gun. A gun can be fired from a long distance without the owner being seen. It almost sounds cowardly. Young Japanese people like collar-length hair like the Vikings of old, but they are not brave at all, unlike the Vikings. Many Japanese military warriors who had brave spirits died after firearms were brought into the wars. There were many, many deaths.

Hatsumi: What are your thoughts on how the *bushi* [warriors] viewed death?

Foreigner: Death is the end of everything. I would rather think about being alive than dying. Death creates nothing.

Hatsumi: However, consider the Japanese *bushi* who was pleased to die in service of his lord. These acts resemble the Christian behavior of a virtuous death in holy war, which offered divine approval and entry to heaven, even in times of severe religious persecution. Even the Vikings were known to run into the midst of their enemies screaming, "May the gods bless us," which brought them brave deaths.

Foreigner: Well, I can understand the idea, but only partially.

* * * * * * * *

On March 1, *Showa* 47 [1972], Mr. Willem Ruska visited me with his brother Martin. It was his opinion that judo is a sport.

Hatsumi: I appreciate that you are practicing judo hard by recognizing it as a sport. However, only a few Japanese judo practitioners define it as a type of sport. Incidentally, what are your thoughts on traditional Japanese *budô*?

Ruska: I am not very familiar with traditional Japanese martial arts. It seems to me to be a very deep, dangerous, and difficult path. It would be difficult for me to continue its practice for a long period.

After I heard this answer, I realized he was a very honest person. He won the Gold medal in two classes, Heavy and Open weight competitions, at the Munich Olympic games [1972]. His victory shocked the people who practice judo in Japan. Yes, I was speaking with that person. His insight and common sense made him the number one judo athlete in the world. I watched his back as he departed, and I immediately knew he would win a world championship title. It was because his knees seemed very soft and flexible like a spring.

IDENTIFICATION OF SPIRITS, CONQUEST OF GHOSTS

What is the true nature of the spiritual world? This is a metaphysical question. Recently, I have begun to ponder the nature of the spiritual world and to attempt to understand its true nature. I find myself defining it as a study in sensitivity, all the while researching it from two differing views: one that affirms the existence of spirits and one that does not. I approach this study in a serious manner in order to sense the spirits (who are by their very nature elusive) by carefully using the six human senses that are to see, hear, smell, touch, etc.

I began my study by recalling that Takamatsu *sensei* once wrote about the spirit world in the magazine ***Meeting and Connecting,*** and immediately began examining it:

> *An overly simplified definition of the spiritual world would be that it is filled with consciousness. This consciousness belongs to a variety of spirits that are the consciousness of god, the consciousness of a wanderer, etc. It is very difficult to clarify them by human comprehension. However, they can be generally classified into seven groups by examining contemporary ideas and modern examples:*

Shin Rei	*divine spirit*
Shihai Rei	*leader spirits*
So Rei	*spirits of ancestors*
Syugo Rei	*protector spirits*
Rei Kon	*central spirits*
Rei Bai	*emissary spirits*
Ja Rei	*wandering spirits*

> *These are the seven kinds of spirits. They can be explained as* **Nenpa**, *waves of consciousness.* ***Ja Rei*** *are explained as not having a proper place in the spirit world. They are best defined as wandering spirits. Spirits of this kind are unidentifiable and include those that are sinister and spiteful. Nonetheless, they are considered powerful enough to make mystical events happen. However,* ***Ja Rei*** *are also known to help people. For instance, people have enough training and intelligence to be a part of our society but sometimes choose to be wanderers. Similarly, some spirits are wandering because they have enough ability but unfortunately, do not have duty to perform. Therefore, it is difficult to say that all wandering spirits are vicious.*

> ***Rei Bai*** *have their place in the spirit world and tend to connect one spirit to another.*

***Rei Kon** originally refers to the center of the spirit world. In this case, it refers to spirits who gather in the center.*

***Syugo Rei** refers to the spirits who protect other spirits or the bodies of creatures for them. They can be thought of as the subconsciousness.*

***So Rei** refers to the noble spirits of our ancestors. However, some of these spirits exist in the world of the wandering spirits.*

***Shihai Rei** refers to the essential spirits who rule other spirits.*

***Shin Rei** is the most fundamental part of the unshaped awareness (God).*

*In this spiritual world, the viscera of **Rei Bai** and **Rei Kai** are called **Yu Kai**. In those spirits, the essence of human beings is called **Rei Kon**. The spirits of animals are known as **Rei Mi**. The spirits of fishes are called **Rei Ki**. The spirits of insects are called **Rei-Mi**. The spirits of woods, stone, mountains, and rivers are known as **Rei-Ku**. The spirits of the gods are called **Ki Rei**.*

[Takamatsu *sensei*]

One day I received a letter with a photograph taken when I had been lecturing and demonstrating *ninjutsu* at the press club. The letter was as follows:

"Dear Mr. Hatsumi:

After finding your address in the newspaper ***Mainichi Shinbun***, I decided to send you this letter. Last year, I was quite impressed when I watched the TV program in which you and Mr. Ishikawa appeared. Later, I was fortunate enough to be at your foreign press club lecture.

Enclosed you will find a photograph I took during this time. It is a pity the picture is not very clear. The room was a bit dark and I did not use a flash bulb. However, notice the *shido rei* [guardian spirit] beside your ear. It seems to be Mr. Chosokabe, a general of the Toyotomi family, who was clean-shaven and in his fifties. Some people might say this picture is just a blur, but I must disagree. His face seems so clear to me.

Whatever your criticism is, I believe there are people who have supernatural abilities. If we should meet again, I will try to take a clearer picture of the spirit. I have heard that *budô* masters can concentrate quicker than other masters, so perhaps if I can concentrate at the same moment, we will be able to better capture the spirit's image."

I immediately decided to visit this person and discuss this spirit. The conversation we had was as follows:

Hatsumi: Thank you for your letter and photograph. How did you shoot the photograph?

Photographer: You exhaled as you threw a *shuriken* and, at that moment, I exhaled and took the photograph.

Hatsumi: In your letter you wrote that the spirit in the picture is the war general Chosokabe. How did you know that?

Photographer: I looked very closely at the photograph. As I did so, I was able to see his spirit and the word 'Chosokabe.' I have a talent for seeing spirits. There was more writing but I could not read it.

Hatsumi: That is truly something. You said the spirit of Chosokabe is with me. To tell the truth, I have found secret writings from the Chosokabe family in a *denshô* book my late teacher gave me.

Photographer: You see! There is a relationship.

Hatsumi: Is there only one spirit nearby someone?

Photographer: No. If you were doing another *bujutsu,* a different spirit might appear in the photograph. If I had a chance, I would like to take its picture.

Hatsumi: If you should see it, please do take its picture.

A few days after I met the photographer, I visited a friend of mine, Soya, who is a doctor and a novelist. I told him of my conversation and that my *shido rei* is the general Chosokabe. I spoke with him:

Hatsumi: What do you think about spirits? Several days ago, someone said the spirit of Isobe was wandering around with Yukio Mishima. [Famous novelist who committed *seppuku*.]

Soya: It is difficult for me to believe in spirits and the like because I have studied the natural sciences for so long. However, I do believe in the concept of *Rinne*, the cycle of reincarnation.

Hatsumi: I must say that I am torn between belief and disbelief.

Recently, I called Masaaki Ishikawa and we spoke about spiritual-photographs. I asked if there could be any trick to it. He said, "If you change the way the film is developed, or the exposure settings, there would surely be a blur."

I sent the photo to Mr. Ishikawa and waited for his reply: "I have seen the photograph and the image is clearly just a blur of light. You can see the three ceiling spotlights reflecting off of you."

Living creatures as well as human beings lose instinct and awareness of their subconscious, as the level of culture becomes greater and greater. Finally, we lose this intuition that is so essential for living.

I remember that once when I shot photographs of the waterfalls at Nikko, a TV program used some of them because there seemed to be faces of dead people that appeared on the pictures. I suppose they were also reflections that were created in the mist by the sunlight.

Few people understand the true nature of the spiritual world. Some religious organizations exploit their believers through these mysteries. When these groups act in this manner, they cease to be worthy religions. My teacher, Takamatsu *sensei*, used to say the following:

"*Gintsu ryoku*, supernatural power, is not a skill or deception. It exists in your heart, through your genuineness. Religion is the same."

One who uses a skill that causes *Ja Nen* or *Aku Nen* [evil consciousness] and deceives people, might themselves be a devil. A religion should never cheat or exploit people. It must be trustworthy.

I believe that having a sincere heart will help each individual to sense and connect with their individual spirit. Otherwise, we will not be able to overcome the "harmful spirits."

I believe that there are spirits. There seem to be too many people in this world who have no spirit or soul. I hope they will live their lives more energetically by finding their own spirits.

THE WORLD OF CRAZINESS

People studying the martial arts are inclined to believe they have a righteous philosophy. They often act imposing. Do common people act this way? Up until recently, I was called "*Bukyo*" [*budô* fanatic]. I cautioned everyone that I was an eccentric person.

One day I was watching a TV talk show that guest-starred a martial art novelist. The novelist, who looked as though he knew little of the martial arts, was quite frail, but was speaking as if he had been a great swordmaster. Some novelists are too quick to act like master swordsmen. I do not know if they have ego problems or if it is a problem with the mass media.

Since most of these novelists do not study or train in the martial arts, they cannot talk with a true understanding of the martial arts or movements, and yet, some interrupt professionals who are studying or training in the martial arts. These people are egomaniacs. I wonder why the mass media helps these amateur critics become "*sensei*" of certain arts. This is a crazy world.

I have listened to numerous writers, researchers, stuntmen, and martial artists dispute *mutô dori* [unarmed sword catch] scenes in the NHK television series ***Haru no Saka Michi***. You risk your life in doing *mutô dori* against a real sword. A poem describes the determination and essence of *mutô*:

Hell under the sword which is raised,
Just step in and there will be heaven.

When you face the sword, you need courage. A person who cannot display true courage normally shows false courage [insanity] by using liquor or drugs. I once had a discussion with a martial artist:

Martial artist: Hatsumi-*san,* I have met many *sensei*, but most are too rigid.

Hatsumi: You mean harassment maniacs and those who are too worried about winning and losing?

Martial artist: Yes. Exactly.

Hatsumi: When I see my teacher, Takamatsu *sensei,* I can tell that the martial artist's affliction, of thinking too much, can be dulled through diligent training. *Sensei* says he achieved this because of his senility, but he is quite healthy and strong.

There are times when a martial artist can become crazy, such as with egomania, an inferiority complex, paranoia, or hypersensitivity (which makes you believe someone is attempting to harm you). For instance, if you were to become an egomaniac, you might think you were strong, almost a hero. An inferiority complex may come when you keep losing and it will make you think you are not good at all or that you do not have the talent to be a martial artist. Paranoia makes you think your opponent looks stronger and causes you to think of how you may be thrown, hit, cut, and killed. Hypersensitivity makes you think somebody is trying to attack you because you have numerous openings [*suki*]. In the process of training, we all come to have one or more of these *illnesses*. Only a balanced individual can exist in this "world of craziness" and move beyond it to become a true master.

It is said that, long ago, a *kensei* [sword saint] needed to learn Zen. However, there was a dark period of Zen in the history of Japan. The priest Ikkyu, who lived during that period, scorned aristocratic authority. Ikkyu called himself "*fukyo*" [crazy]. He interpreted craziness and courage as the same thing. One day, Shogun Ashikaga visited Ikkyu to amend some outdated laws. Other priests started to fidget and tremble because of the Shogun's presence, but Ikkyu took off his hat, stood at a place higher than the Shogun and was prepared to offer it to the Shogun. One of the Shogun's followers was furious and put his hand on the hilt of his sword, readying to draw it, but then stopped before he shed blood near a Buddhist alter. Instead, he lunged out with his hand to receive the hat for the Shogun. Ikkyu said, "I cannot give this to an attendant. I will only give it directly to the Shogun." I bet you cannot imagine how surprised everyone watching was! This is an example of courage with humor.

There are many forms of this *kyo* [craziness]. The form of spirit: a person who desires changing techniques or seeks varying teachers. The form of depressiveness: a person who smiles [gets gratification] after attacking someone. The form of distraction: the person who attacks the opponent's territory. The form of the intoxicated: a person who cannot hold the sword without alcohol, etc. Anyone who becomes "deluded" from this craziness and then returns to a sensible state will become a true expert. In addition, I inform my students to be mindful of being a bit schizophrenic or split personality, so that through mental concentration they will be aware enough to sense opponents in every direction.

THE EVOLUTION OF FIGHTING TECHNIQUE

The fighting arts were born along with the birth of humanity. However, styles that are taught now probably began after the Komatsu Emperor (1392-1413). The system of passing the martial arts down through the generations changed from *kuden* [oral transmissions] to *makimono*.

The names of the *ryu* [schools] were not instantly applied; long periods of time passed before they became recognized, and they were then called by the names of the places [where they originated] or by the founder's name. I believe the reason why some were called "*hô*" and not "*ryu*" was because they were referred to by the names of the places where they originated. This was often easier to understand and more convenient for the common people. Usually, when a tradition is named after the founder, it was not named while he was still alive.

For example, Tsukahara Bokuden was applied to many martial arts traditions after his death. Similarly, *Togakure ryu ninpô* was named by the third generation Togakure Goro.

Many scrolls list the origin of their tradition as bestowed by heaven or Buddha. This may imply that people cannot be genuine martial artists unless they study with acceptance of this religion. The methods of passing down this information were by writing, drawing, and *kuden* [oral teachings]. The written methods often contained hidden meanings. This was not just to encourage you to learn from your teacher but was also for keeping the scrolls from being decoded too easily should they be stolen. Therefore, even if you found a *makimono* you would not be able to understand its full meaning unless you were an expert in its teachings. Some older *makimono* were written with ancient letters on cryptomeria bark, but these scrolls, which are viewable to this day, are very fine ones with letters, drawings, and fine artwork on paper. These scrolls have different symbols and lettering depending upon the era they were written in and the customs of those who wrote them. A person who learned foreign strategy from Chinese scrolls would rearrange it in the Japanese style. A person like this, with high regard for traditional Japanese ideas, may have transferred scrolls like the ***Amatsu Tatara Hibun*** into a more generalized Japanese scroll. Older *makimono* hinted at the *shinden*, divine enlightenment, though their usage. Since the gods had inspired these scrolls, understanding them would lead to spiritual enlightenment.

A *budôka* who studied the consciousness of god, recognized the tradition's patron deity, and studied and trained in their martial art, were permitted into the inner secrets. These inner secrets came from lessons in *kuden* [oral transmissions], *denshô* [written transmissions], *shinden* [mental transmission], and the *shinden* [divine transmission] in the *ryu*. Only after fully comprehending these lessons could a person read and fully understand the scrolls of the *ryu*. Therefore, even if the scrolls were stolen, it would not mean the true tradition was stolen. The scrolls were symbols of the martial art.

One martial art history researcher examined many martial art traditions over a period of several years and came to realize the pointlessness of his objectives. A person who has not studied and trained with great dedication cannot succeed in such research.

Occasionally, in some of the older *makimono*, we find that a 3rd, 4th or 14th *sôke*'s name was omitted because a proper successor did not emerge. In many of these cases, people calling themselves successors have emerged to "inherit" the martial tradition. There is no hope for these people to be genuine martial artists.

Modern military combat has changed from the time of the *bô* [staff] and stone to the time of the nuclear bomb. This is the same basic concept as in how *hikiriusus*, *hikirikine*, and *hikiuchi'ishi* [stones such as flint] developed into butane lighters. The splendid thing about Japanese *budô* is that many traditions have developed extensive mental and physical training by adding traditional customs.

A foreign professor scrutinized the Japanese people in this way: "The Japanese race is a nation that consumes rice. These people will progress if they are given proper counseling. There is great virtue in the Japanese people. On the other hand, they have a failing in that they are too moderate in their developments. A good example of this is the battleship **Yamato** that was something of which they were quite proud, but was built too late, in the time of the airplane [bomber]."

This scholar identified the conservative and irrational characteristics of some Japanese. Their views are understandable and valid in some ways, but fallible as history show has shown. Their mistakes were derived from individualism and poor judgment. They chose not to include many experts in the design process. Furthermore, many of those who became famous because of the ship's construction were not very deserving.

To fight against an opponent is not the highest achievement of the martial arts. Likewise, those who have won many competitions are not necessarily the greatest martial artists. A sincere martial artist has to keep training, be steadfast to changes that occur or the passage of time, and live with an eagerness for *budô* as his base.

In the period of the Emperor Tenchi Tenno [c. 650], *bushi* were sometimes chosen from farmers who were healthy and could endure strain. This is why the true form of the character ***bu*** is written with the character **genuine**. They did not merely choose the strong and those that loved to fight. The way of the soldier, the way of the martial artist, the way of the bowyer, the way of the archer... in this fashion, sayings changed with the passage of time, but the essence of each remained: this is the *true path*. Many *bushi* were sheltered and educated in an honorable manner by their feudal lords. Nevertheless, I feel the true achievements were accomplished by the masterless *bushi* with extraordinary spirits.

THE JAPANESE SWORD AND BUDÔ

The Japanese sword is considered a thing of splendor because it has a soul. This soul is a product of the swordmaker who endures perspiration, austerity, and suffering. The soul is intensified when the red glowing blade is plunged into water. The sword's essence is then increased with the joy of the swordsman who takes ownership of the blade from the swordsmith. Thus, is created the life energy of the Japanese sword.

The creation of a sword can be compared with the growth of a human being. In the beginning, there is only the raw material of scattered iron ore. After being subjected to many tempering sessions, a blade is eventually created. If, however, the blade is not tempered by a great swordmaker, it turns out to be a dull thing of little strength or distinction. That which is created by a master artist is, on the other hand, an article of purity and magnificence. Beyond its creation, the sword improperly cared for will be reduced to rust. Occasional powdering and oiling is necessary to keep it in peak condition.

It was natural for a warrior to be rebuked for not taking respectable care of his sword. Likewise, human beings must be urged to cultivate an attitude of polishing themselves and achieve tempering from facing hardships. The warrior aspirant incapable of such disciplined evolution will never become an exceptional "sword."

A sword does not exist for the exclusive purpose of cutting people open. No matter how great the sword, its use can result in a notched edge or a finish spoiled by blood chemicals. A swordsman's poem remarks:

Victory without unsheathing the blade.
If you must draw the sword, do not cut.
Merely endure.
Comprehend the profound
Consequences of taking any life.

The cutting method employed in ancient times was to extend and push with the action of the cut. However, in the third month of *Meiji* 27 (1895), the Japanese military force reformed their traditional *kendô* sword arts. The military leaders adopted the single-handed ceremonial sword of the modern times. Along with the altered sword design there came the inward pulling, swing cut.

In an actual sword fight, this pulling cut is an excessively dangerous action. Imagine a scene where your adversary is attacking you with a downward cut. At that moment, suppose you cut across his mid-section with the pull-cut. He would then be forced forward to cut you straight down. If you cut his torso with a push-cut when he was to strike down on top of your head, he would be thrown backwards, and you would triumph. The sword methods of such movies as ***Zatoichi*** or ***Mekura no Oichi*** are called *katate giri* [single-handed cut]. This can also be done if the sword has a narrow blade and if the wielder knows how to cut with proper body motion.

Since we use a sword with a blade length of one *shaku* four *sun* to eight *sun* [approx. 18 to 22.5 inches] in *ninpô,* there are *kata* such as *hidari katate giri* and throwing *metsubushi* [blinding powder] to escape.

It is not necessary to behead an enemy in order to kill him. Human beings can be mortally wounded with small cuts such as a slash across the carotid artery. Those people whose cutting does not incorporate the knowledge of vulnerable points into their swordwork should have their technique called "*wood chopping sword methods*."

The length of the *katana* was approximately three *shaku* [three feet]. Some people wonder how they can swing around a three *shaku* sword. These same people believe that a sword is swung through arm strength alone. These people need to understand that a long sword is manipulated through proficient body motion and through reaction to various movements.

In the *denshô* of *Kukishin ryu*, it says that on New Year's Day of *Engen* 3 [1338], when Ashikaga Takauji led his large army to Kyoto, Taro Takehide of Kangun confronted Yashiro Gonnosuke Ujisato of Batsugun with a spear. Ujisato's weapon was a big, sword three *shaku* long, and the power of it was rumored to be capable of cutting down a large tree. When Takehide thrust his *yari* [spear] at Ujisato, his spear was struck in two, leaving only the handle in his hands. When Ujisato tried to cut in without a moments delay, Takehide used the technique of "*rai'un*." His handle flashed the sunlight, so he blinded his opponent and was able to knock down Ujisato and take his head.

The sword has changed through historical periods. It began as a stone object, and later took forms in bronze and then steel. In ancient times, a wooden sword is believed to have been adapted. Loquat was the principal wood used, and the length was approximately three feet with a curved end for gripping. Primitive sword fighting methods developed from this wooden club-sword.

Nevertheless, if you train in *bôjutsu* against a three *shaku* sword, it is certain you can understand the real meaning of *tôhô* [sword methods]. This is where body motion and *mutô* [no sword], the sense of you yourself becoming a sword, would be clearly understood.

Someone once asked me, "How many people could be cut open with a sword before the blade would begin to corrode? After five cuts, wouldn't the blade be affected from contact with body oils and fluids?" What silliness!

A sword involves a lot more than the blade cutting an opponent. A sword has "hands," "legs," "head," and "body"—just like a human being. You must be able to use the whole of the weapon and all its parts (such as the hilt, cord, scabbard, etc.) effectively. You must then learn to wield the blade while cutting, thrusting, striking, punching, throwing and receiving wristlocks, cuts and take downs. After learning all these, then for the first time you would know the sword method of power called "*nuki kazu kate*" [win without drawing the sword]. Then you would certainly comprehend the *gokui* of *mutô*.

ABOUT KIAI

Words can be used to harm as well as to benefit people. There is a special vitality and mystical quality in words. With one word a person can be struck discourteously or even, lose a political office. Thus, by knowing how to use a word, you can either extinguish or enliven a person.

This means we have to consider the art of conversation as a form of strategy. To illustrate, the deliberation between Katsu Kaishu and Saigo Takamori saved the people of Japan. [Kaishu, a Shogunate representative, and Takamori, leader of the Imperial forces, are credited with negotiating a peaceful end to feuding and the beginning of the Meiji Restoration.]

Talking and shouting [*kiai*] has to originate from one's *hara* [abdomen]. Conversation without courage or sincerity could easily causes quarreling. Likewise, if a *kiai* did not come from one's *hara*, it would be weak and lack fortitude.

A judge in a courtroom is like a leader in chaos. He decides people's lives within the context of their comments. He must use his *hara* when talking. Hiroshi Itsuki, who was the defense lawyer in the Yakkai case, had a talent for speaking and a spirit that let him give a very passionate defense. It spurred the idea that people's lives cannot be taken away by power. Ultimately, he won his case. It was definitely his *hara* and his spirit that allowed him to win.

One written theory in the *denshô* scrolls, concerning *kiai,* states, "When breathing changes into *kiai,* this is known as *sansei fushin."* This proposes that there cannot be an articulation unless three types of *kiai* are mixed. When all three are together in the mind, it becomes an intention. *Sansei* refers to the three different kinds of *kiai.*

The first *kiai* is that of winning. It makes the opponent feel defeated while removing his strength to attack. We call this *kangi yaku.*

The second *kiai* proclaims to the opponent that you are about to attack. This causes him to think he has an unguarded point [*suki*], which you are about to exploit. He loses confidence, causing him to feel anxious, and results in further *suki.*

The third *kiai* is deceptive in that it announces to the opponent that you know what he is about to do. Since you perform this *kiai* right before he attacks you, the opponent becomes perplexed and exposes *suki.* Then you can attack these openings and win!

There is also a voiceless *kiai* and a shadow *kiai.* These two are a mixture of the previously described *kiai* and render the opponent's fighting skills useless.

When you are going to attack, you perform the heartfelt *kiai* of *kangi yaku,* which is "YA!" The next *kiai* if that of *haku yakuso,* which is "AH!" After you know which trick your opponent is going to use, you give out the deceptive *kiai,* which is "TOH!" This is the third *kiai,* the *kiai* of *yaku sohei.* When these three are together, you give the immovable, truly silent *kiai* of "UM!" This *kiai* is also known as *mitsu kujiku* [three breaks]. The first break is the disrupting of the opponent's spirit. The second is the fracturing of the opponent's technique. In addition, the third break is that of shattering the opponent's body. When these three are blended together, they generate the *kiai* of *fudo kanashibari* [immobilizing and binding of an opponent].

Takamatsu *sensei* once related a story about this "overwhelming" of an opponent's spirit. One day, when Takamatsu *sensei* was training at Toda *sensei*'s *dojo,* a person doing *musha shugyo* entered their *dojo* and said, "I have been studying *Sekiguchi ryu* and have heard about Mr. Toda. I would like to challenge your school." Takamatsu *sensei* received permission from Toda *sensei* and let the challenger into the *dojo.* When it was time for the match, one of Toda's students [named Ossan] came forward and declared that he wanted to be the first to fight the challenger. During this time in Japan, it was an unwritten policy to have a senior student, someone young and strong, as the first defender. Although he had a good body and a scar on his face that made him look tough, Ossan was almost 38 years old and lacking in fighting ability and martial skill. Takamatsu *sensei* had thought he himself would be the first to fight the challenger, but Ossan would not withdraw. Takamatsu *sensei* finally gave up trying to dissuade Ossan and let him fight first.

Ossan walked bravely to the center of the *dojo.* Challenger and defender bowed to each other, stepped apart, and stared at each other. Suddenly, Ossan went to attack. His eyes became fierce, his face looked like that of a demon and he stamped his foot as if to break the floor. All the while Ossan was shouting "YA!" as he moved forward to attack. His opponent, the *Sekiguchi ryu* man, retreated about two meters and said, "I give up." The match was over and Toda *sensei* asked the opponent, "What happened?" He answered, "I am sorry, but his strong and fearful *kiai* made me unable to attack."

This *Sekiguchi ryu* man had already lost to Ossan the use of his mental power. It should not be like this in the martial arts. To be a martial artist one needs *banpen fugyo,* which is the ability to swiftly adapt to changes in technique and environment. Martial artists should not be afraid of such changes. It is important to develop a spirit to enable one to act calmly in all situations. To train the spirit is the real value of learning the martial arts and the skill of *kiai.*

If you can master these, then your conversations will be more interesting and you will be able to gracefully work through your problems. There would be no need for hostility. This thinking can even improve your communication skills.

CHAPTER TWO

WORLD OF BUDÔ AND NINPÔ

THE DENSHÔ LIVES

Japanese history has been influenced most notably through the ***Kojiki*** and ***Nihon-shoki*** [7th century historical writings]. I have a great interest in these books because the secrets of *budô* and the *denshô* are written in *kamiyomoji* [7th century "script of the gods"] also.

There are several theories about *kamiyomoji*. One theory is that there are ten or more kinds of *kamiyomoji*. A second theory is that these writings transformed from Sanskrit. Yet, another theory is that there were no such letters, and Hirata Atsutame fabricated them. The scholars that study the *Uetsu fumi* [old writings found in Uetsu province] say there are Kuki, Izumo, Wamoji, Abe, Kiyohara, Moriya, Nakatomi, Ohtomo, Mononobe, Shinma, Kasuga, Takeuchi, Fuji *bunsho*, etc [styles of writing]. Some scholars are studying these writing styles. To me, it does not matter which ones are legitimate because my purpose is to unravel *ango* [secret codes] or to study the strategy of ninja through *kamiyomoji*.

Both *Yagyu ryu* and *Kuki ryu* were influenced by the ***Tenshin Hibun***, which in turn was influenced by *kamiyomoji*, too. For example, in one of the *denshô* it states, "this is based on *ootomo shuku kojitsu tenshin bi to kai wa sei shu shin den soku chi shizen ryoku* which is a religion and *bumon no michi* [*budô*]. There are four scrolls in the ***Hikan Tora no Maki*** [secret scrolls of the tiger]. And there are two sets of ***Ryu no Maki*** [scrolls of the dragon], a set containing eight scrolls and another containing twelve." There are many portions of their secret verses left written in *kamiyomoji*. Descriptions of ninjutsu are found in the ***Ryusen no Maki*** [scroll of the concealed clear sound].

As I wrote before, in Japan around 500 B.C. there was a record written in *kamiyomoji* about the first battle between Chinese Buddhists, who had come to Japan, and the Japanese dynasty.

Kumiuchi [grappling], *bô* [staff], and *sekito* [stone throwing] were used to fight against the enemy, and ditch digging was used to keep opponents at a distance. It is a fact that *kamiyomoji* has had a strong influence over *budô*. In addition, it is fun to figure out the writer's personality and the degree of his martial arts training through judging his writing and the quality of the work. Sometimes it is moving to find and share their recollections of training. Each time I read one of the *denshô,* I feel like I practice with these old martial arts masters.

If I read it for four hours, I get just as tired as if I practiced with the warriors that wrote them. The teachers who wrote the books are not dead; they remain vigorously alive through their writings. I am convinced that the spirits of the teachers that contributed to the *denshô* never fade away, but stay powerful forever.

FROM NINPÔ TO NINJUTSU

Ninpô began as training to become a moral people and to learn to endure in whatever social condition one is in; to know and accept one's fate, and to live for human beings and all other creatures. The person who masters all of these is a ninja.

There are numerous cases of petty people losing their common sense in order to keep up with our constantly changing world. These people forgot how to endure and grew smug about their talent and technique, or were obsessed with standing out in society. Let me explain practical ninjutsu here. It is called *tongyo no jutsu*.

Each *ton* [evasion method] has an *omote* [outer] and an *ura* [inner] side. For example, while wood, fire, soil, metal, and water are "outer views," they are paired with people, birds, animals, insects, and fish as "inner views." Other *ton* are heaven, earth, and man. There are a total of 30 different methods. This implies that the ninja can use anything to his benefit.

Tongyo is called *tonkyo* in Buddhism. When you use *tongyo*, you must have a keen sense of intuition. [*Tonkyo* means reaching nirvana without basic training.] A person who desires this must chant the magic spells of *kuji* and *juji* [nine words or ten words].

Ninpô is also called *nigeru jutsu* [running away method] or *sakeru jutsu* [avoidance method], but it never means running away in defeat. Both Kusunoki Masashige and Mao [Tse Tung] finally won by running and hiding from a situation. Now, we begin with introducing the methods of *suiton no jutsu*:

Suiton no Jutsu

Suiton no jutsu uses the characteristics of water as a special material for you to gain an advantage. First, the swimming method of *suiton* is called *aori-hira*. The practice starts from learning how to swim without making a sound. Of course, there is a method to make sound intentionally, to draw the enemy's attention. The next lesson involves swimming under various conditions such as between drifting logs, or in fog, rain, or snow.

Then the practice proceeds with how to walk on water. This involves walking on ladders or poles in the water; actually, it looks like magic or a miracle. There is a way to deceive the enemy's eyes regarding the depth of the water using *mizugumo* [tool named after water spider], which is a bag made of horse skin. I had thought this was a Japanese invention but have found that Assyrian soldiers used a sheepskin to execute a surprise attack against their enemies.

When submerged in water you breathe through a hollow bamboo tube about four feet long. They use items such as *hasamibume*, bamboo, reed, logs, *tsuzura* [a plant], barrels, rafts, and boats to float on the water. There is a wonderful device called *shinobigai*. It was made with bamboo and a bamboo fan with a weight attached. [Used for rowing.]

In general, humans are apt to indulge in desires. They say there are 84,000 temptations for us. Then there must be 84,000 ways of *suiton no jutsu* to avoid drowning. [Double meaning suggests drowning in water and drowning in personal desires.]

Mokuton no jutsu

These methods involve hiding behind trees, cutting down wood, and making noise by shaking branches to get the enemy's attention. In *Togakure ryu*, they use *ryuton no jutsu* [dragon escape methods]: climbing trees using *tekagi* [hand claws] or *ashikagi* [foot claws]. There is also *ippon sugi nobori no jutsu* [solitary cedar climbing methods]. There is a way to do *mokuton* [wood evasion] using *kama yari* [sickle spear] or *shinobi nawa* [rope]. The legendary hero Sarutobi Sasuke also was said to use *shinobi nawa* when he would soar through the trees. Have you read about the scroll called ***Ryuko***? *Ryu* [dragon] symbolizes the victory and *ko* [tiger] symbolizes the ability to sense the enemy. The ninja were called "crow with three legs." This meant they ran fast, their assisting leg was strong, and their hands were swift. They could also perceive danger before it neared and were able to evade potential harm. These are three important basics of *tongyo:* Be articulate and handy, have swift legs, and master *bôjutsu*.

Katon no jutsu

Regarding the relationship between humans and fire, I think that humans' stamina has decreased since we started to cook food by fire. When you consider the gas lighter, you realize people used to use *hiuchi ishi* [striking rocks to create fire], and now they use a gas lighter. If you think of a gas lighter's fire as "a new fire," and act childish then you may be burned. On this point, animals know the danger of fire better than humans do. It seems that people no longer understand the primitive senses of small creatures. Fire is the passion of life. *Katon*'s early lessons commence with *do no hi*. An *uchitake* [hand warmer] was used to set fire to fallen leaves or *shoji* [screen doors] while ninja hid behind them. Long ago there was a mysterious technique called *onibi*, which involved wearing a demon mask and blowing fire out of the mouth through a bamboo stick. Progression in the lessons of *katon* begins with the use of gunpowder. Then there are *oozutsu* [wooden cannon], *hozutsu* [wooden bazooka], *sodezutsu* [bamboo gun], *totetsu ho* [grenade], *umebi* [mine], *bakuhatsuya* [rocket], *higurumaken* [*shuriken* wrapped with gunpowder], *kaen kusarigama* [*kusarigama* striking bomb]. They [ninja] use gunpowder not only for its explosive power, but they also use a special kind that produces a lot of smoke, which can change color or be mixed with poison. They use seven-colored smoke for signaling each other from a distance. Furthermore, the ninja knew how to put out fire using water in hidden gourds. This was called *tsuri hozuki.*

Doton no jutsu

There are nuclear weapons all over the world, and many countries are developing such bombs. In Sweden, they have a shelter to use in case of nuclear attack. Should they need it, they will hide underground. For the ninja, *doton* [earth evasion] means to hide under soil or pebbles or behind boulders. The ninja also used rocks, stones, and sand to attack the enemy's eyes and body. *Otoshiana* [pit trap] is also a kind of weapon. Sometimes, the ninja hid in the pit. *Baken do* is an empty boulder made of clay and fallen leaves in which ninja hid. They would dig tunnels under this rock and use *datto no jutsu* [escape like a rabbit] to disappear. They confused their enemies with the sounds of footsteps or, with diversionary footprints, or they used ninja *wari ashi* [*see* **Footwork Reveals Your Mind and Body**] or made their footprints appear like an animal's. When they did not do *warashi*, they somersaulted down, letting only their heels leave an impression as they landed. They could use *doton* with the swirling winds and dust to get away. It can be used in conjunction with heavy rains. Thus, they arranged each *tongyo* with other factors to enhance their effects. They improvised. There are other *doton no jutsu* that use caltrops or *kunai* [knife-like weapon].

Kinton no jutsu

This technique focuses on using reflected light or sound against the enemy's eyes and ears. It was used to get the enemy's attention by luring him with gold and treasures. One could poison the enemy with metallic substances. In the old days, the mirrors were not made of glass, but rather of metal. The ninja used these to blind his enemy with reflected sunlight or to send signals. Concealed, he could use these to see an enemy's reflection. They were also used as hidden weapons.

Humans have a weakness for gold and treasures. Such a *bushi* was called a "filthy officer." During the European Middle Ages, knights put diamonds in their weapons to avoid poison. [Superstition that diamonds gather wetness when they approach poison.] Ninja had a similar superstition that required coral because coral decays when it gets close to poison. Ninja also use "golden words" [flattery] in a disguise; they knew chemistry well, and freely manipulated human senses.

Kunoichi

Women can also use sex as a tool. *Kunoichi* [female ninja] use it as a secret weapon. They used their femininity to blind male opponents, to crush their enemy's *suzu* [bells], and used their unique abilities to entwine illusion and reality in the mind's of their foes.

There are 48 *manko no jutsu* [wholehearted methods]. Forty-eight means everything from a good sword [*meito*] to any good weapon [*meiki*] and are words used by common men. However, the ninja used any kind of dull sword or dull weapon, just like Kobo Daishi [famous priest known for beautiful calligraphy]. He did not fuss about the type of writing brush he used. The *kunoichi* also excelled at ground techniques [sex]. They were well versed in a myriad of lovemaking techniques and knew more than most modern therapists. An English spy and Richard Sorge both said women do not make good spies. However, women such as Mata Hari and Keeler acted well as *kunoichi*. A *kunoichi* cannot be hysterical or too emotional. They must have strong *kage* [hidden] power. *Kage* also means "*kage*" [covert part].

Choyakujutsu

This phrase expresses the ability to swiftly move away from your opponent. *Shinobi* learn *tobi roppo* [six-directional leaping] and with these lessons, you must be able to leap off in any direction. The term *kyushaku takatobi* [nine-foot high jump] is from ancient times when nine was considered the highest number. Therefore, this meant to leap as high as you could. In addition, *habatobi sangen* means to leap with the timing or rhythm of one, two, and three.

There are various ways to practice leaping high. For example, a ninja would plant some flax seeds or use bamboo shoots and jump over them each day, as they grew higher. However, a human being's jumping ability does have a limit. Therefore, ninja invented ways to jump higher using the *bô, shinobi* sword, or a long ladder. Each *ryuha* devised its own special methods.

The ninja had used a special ladder to sneak into houses from a tree. Rather than jumping over fences, the *shinobi* sword was used for peering over the fence by placing one foot on the sword guard.

There is an unusual technique to fling or leap sideways, as if flying. Ninja used this for *shinobi gaeshi.* This leap was inspired by how animals hop sideways.

A ninja used a ladder made of women's hair. This hair-rope was strong enough for five heavy men to hang on it. The word *himo* [pimp], meaning a man who lives off a woman's earnings may have originated from this rope idea.

They say ninja could fly on a large kite, but that is not true. The ninja would put a dummy on a kite and make it appear as if he were flying on it. Ninja trained in the art of appearing superhuman, as if they were truly more than simple mortals. They mastered these ingenious skills.

HOJUTSU AND NINJUTSU

At the foreign correspondents' club, they call *budô* an eastern magic. I performed dangerous feats, illusionary arts [*hojutsu*], and *budô* while trying to show and explain the true martial arts to them. Of course, I showed them martial arts trickery alongside real *budô*, so they could understand the difference.

For instance, there is a trick regarding the Japanese sword. I explained, "The Japanese sword is sharpened lengthwise, so if you pull it along your body in a certain way or stand on it, it won't cut." Then I put the blade on my face, tied it on with a rope, and pulled the sword off. Dr. Stecker [translator of Kawabata literature] said, "The sword doesn't cut, it must not be sharp. Let me examine it." So, I threw a bamboo pole in the air and, single-handedly, used the sword to cut it into two pieces.

Sometimes, we see television shows where a man claims to be superhuman. On one such show, the man lived in the mountains and was claiming that he could strike down a flying bird with his *kiai.* This is not possible. The trick is to press both eyes of a bird or hen, flip it upside down, shake it a couple of times, and rub its body. It becomes unconscious temporarily. Then release it in the air, and the bird will fall since it has lost its flying sense. Another trick is to put a frog down on its back and rub its belly with your palm. It will fall asleep.

I see some people use these kinds of sensational tricks to make it seem that they possess amazing powers or that they are masters of *budô*. They just trick us; they are fakes.

At a performance of *kiai jutsu*, "This is a real mandarin orange. It has not had the rind peeled off. Please, someone check it. Okay? Now, let me show you; I will cut up the inside with a powerful *kiai*." Then the performer makes a *kiai* and the inside of the orange is cut in half. This is a total fraud; he has cut the inside of the orange using a needle and thread. Some people use this kind of trick to promote *budô*.

Shishinjutsu [needle methods] means to penetrate the body with a needle without feeling pain or spilling blood. The most important points of this technique are to use a sanitized needle and pick the safest spot in the body and put the needle in with a single swift thrust.

It is a good idea to check the needle first or the technique might fail and you will begin to bleed. Even professional *shishinjutsu* masters feel pain when a bee stings them. The trick is that they choose a single place on their body and develop a callus there before demonstrating the trick. They then apply the needle at that same exact spot. They do not even feel a pinch when they perform their show. In the following section, I will explain some techniques that I demonstrated:

Kairiki Jutsu & Fudo Jutsu

"Step onto my right hand and then grab my waist..." This is what a performer says as he hoists a man onto his shoulders. One-handed! However, this is no amazing feat once I explain. The trick lies in the phrase, "Hold on to my waist." The second person steps up onto the performers arm, leans forward and grabs the performer's waist. By leaning forward, the second man's body weight ends up centered over the performer's shoulder. This same principle can be applied to balancing a desk on your chin as a woman sits on top of it.

Another person stood up and said, "Try picking me up." Another performer easily picked him up. Then the man said, "Try to pick me up again!" This time the second performer could not pick him up. It was as if his feet were held down by weights. This is considered *fudojutsu*, but actually, the person only shifted his center of gravity backward. If someone is trying to pick you up, simply bend forward and put out your arms. That is all you have to do to defeat his attempts.

The next technique is to let a strong man hold one long stick with both his arms straight out in front at chest level. The performer holds one end of a *bô* with his right hand and they start to push each other at the signal. At this moment, the performer lowers his center of gravity and pushes the *bô* upward on an angle. The performer, using only his right hand, will push the strong man backward. This is called dynamics. In *sumo,* the best way to push your opponent is to lower your body with both arms held tightly to your side and push upward toward the opponent. This is the most sensible way to defeat him.

The next technique has the performer holding a six-foot *bô* with only his pinky finger and pushing it toward the opponent whom is pressing forward with full body weight. The contender sees the tip of the *bô* on the performer's pinky, holds the *bô* firmly, and pushes against it knowing that the man's pinky has no strength to stop him. But the performer's pinky does not break or give way! Instead, the opponent is pushed back by the trickster. This is another bit of mischief. The performer creates the illusion that he has placed the *bô* on his pinky but actually, he was pushing the *bô* using his palm right below his middle finger.

Another technique is to pull two cars, which are attached by a chain to your arms. Yet, another trick is to sit between two cars with your legs outstretched and hold the cars in place using only your waist and leg motion. I have omitted the full description of these because I am afraid some silly people without training will try them and become injured.

Nawa Nuke & Tejyo Nuke No Jutsu

They say ninja freed themselves from being bound by dislocating their joints. If a martial artist made his joints too flexible, it could be a terrible disadvantage in real combat. They hardly use the *nawa nuke jutsu* [rope escaping methods]. In the old days, *Nawa nuke* was easy if you followed the lessons your teacher showed you. It is important to choose appropriate rope materials used for tying. Certain ropes are easier to escape from than others are.

The first thing you do if you are tied up is open your hands and loosen the knots by rotating your wrists. Then try to create a gap between your hands and the rope, so you can start to free one hand, thumb first.

Years ago, there was an American master escape artist that could free himself from any type of handcuff but he never revealed his secrets. After he died, they researched his methods and concluded that his wrists were double-jointed. There are ways to get out of handcuffs but I believe that it would not be wise to make this secret public because it could only harm society.

Paralyzing Animals

Did you know that a snake stops moving when you hold its neck with your left hand and squeeze it about three times with your right? Long ago, Miyamoto Musashi was eating at a small teashop, when a scoundrel named Kumosuke came to provoke him. Musashi acted as if he paid Kumosuke no attention, but then, he instinctively used his chopsticks to catch a fly that was moving about his rice. Kumosuke saw this, was dumbfounded, and ran away.

There is a man in Yamato who is said to have fought against a bear and won. When he was attacked, he jumped right onto the bear, thrust his hand into its mouth, twisted its tongue off, and killed it. It should be considered a lucky accident that he survived.

When in China, late one night Takamatsu *sensei* was walking on an old country road with one of his Chinese friends. Suddenly, a few dogs attacked them, the largest one in the pack attacking *sensei*. [It was about the size of a Saint Bernard.] The dog put its forepaws onto *sensei*'s shoulders and began growling. As it was about to bite him, *sensei* stared at the dog and paused motionless with *fudôshin*.

Sensei had learned this from his teacher Toda Shinryuken *sensei* while he was studying ninjutsu. The lesson was that most beasts would not bite you if you do not make any movements. The moment the dog stopped growling, *sensei* struck it with his fist right between the eyes. The dog wailed and, with the other dogs, ran away. This type of counter should only be applied after studying animal behavior.

Method to Step on Needles or Broken Glass

Try to stand barefoot upon ten or more metal plates with nails protruding out of them. You should not be hurt because your weight is dispersed over many nail points. According to this principle, the more nails beneath your feet, the closer they are placed together, the less pain you will feel. This same principle applies to when you stand on broken pieces of glass. Be aware that it is important to pile the pieces close together. The skin on the bottom of your feet is the toughest skin on your whole body. It is also very important to brush off the glass pieces when you step off the pile of glass, because a single piece can easily cut into your sole.

Iaijutsu

"I'm a master of *iaijutsu,*" a performer said demonstrating his ability to strike through chopsticks [*waribashi*] with a paper or break a bamboo stick held up by two loops of paper. This demonstration has absolutely nothing to do with real *iaijutsu*. The performer only used the principles of inertia to create this magical illusion.

For instance, before the demonstration, the performer might say, "I'm going to break ten wooden chopsticks with only one chopstick" and then asks a member of the audience to hold a bunch of chopsticks. The performer strikes through them with a single chopstick while yelling a fierce *kiai.* Instead of the chopstick breaking the other sticks, it is the performer secretly using his index finger to do the break.

Techniques of Using Fire

The hottest point of a candle's flame is the outermost part of the flame. If you know the characteristics of fire, even eating fire seems simple. Once a flame is placed inside your mouth, it disappears instantly because of lack of oxygen and the dampness of your saliva. When performers use heated coals, they bite the ash part with their teeth. There is a remarkable feat called *tekkajutsu* in which the performer rubs the surface of a red-hot iron bar with his bare-hand. When his assistant helps wash the performers hands, it is called *okiyome* [cleanse body before holy ceremony]. This causes a phenomenon that is similar to when you throw water at a hot stove and the water bounces off in little sizzling droplets. With this same idea, the performer's hand is covered with a thin veil of water so it is not burned.

If you put salt on your palms before executing this technique, the salt burns and makes purple smoke. This not only increases your safety but also creates a theatrical effect at the same time. *Hiwateri no jutsu* [walking on hot coals] also applies this principle.

Methods to Control People

There is an illusion in which a performer can make it look like he controls other people with his will. For instance, you can hypnotize someone and make him or her bend their body in a bow-like fashion. Then make a human bridge by putting their feet on one chair and their hands on another. Then sit a person on top of him or set a big stone on his chest. Some performers do *mochi tsuki* [place a big wooden bowl down, and strike into it with a large wooden hammer to make rice cakes] on the person's chest while he is in this position. The trick is to make sure the person arching their back keeps his leg joints straight. This is a principle of *taikobashi* [drum bridge]. There is no need to actually hypnotize the person.

Another simple maneuver is to stand people in line and knock them down using a *kiai.* The trick involves the domino effect or *shogi daoshi no jutsu*. They turn around a few times and hold their arms at an angle. Then they set their weight onto their heels, keep their knees close together and hold their hands straight out in front of them. Then, as they line up, do *kiai.* Since they were all standing in a very unbalanced way, when one person starts to fall, everybody follows. If a person with poor balance were first in line there would not even be a need to vocalize the *kiai* to make them all fall.

Techniques Using a Japanese Sword

As I mentioned earlier in this chapter, the Japanese sword is sharpened lengthwise, so it will not cut you if you step on the blade in a certain way. A performer that can cut a *daikon* on top a man's bare stomach or slide his bare hand along a blade edge surely knows the characteristics of the Japanese sword. When I lectured to the Japanese Prince about ninjutsu, a student in the Gakushu In School played with the sword that I had been using, assuming it was a trick weapon. He touched the sword's tip and actually cut his fingers. As this shows, it is dangerous to try these techniques if you do not know the characteristics of the sword. In addition, it is important to know that knives, razor blades, and kitchen knives are all cut differently and that they cannot be used to do these techniques.

Methods of Hitting, Breaking, and Taking a Hit

One aspect of this trick is that you appear not to feel any pain even if you hit your own arms or body with an iron bar. This involves holding an iron bar in your right hand and hitting your left arm as hard as you can. The trick is that you hit with the section of the bar closest to your hand holding it. The point to strike at is the thickest muscle on the receiving arm. If you were to keep hitting the strongest muscles of your whole body, the iron bar would bend. By applying this principle, you can come to feel indestructible, feeling little pain even if an opponent hits you with a stick or *bô*. You can even bend an iron bar with your knee by applying a similar technique. Some people break glass bottles with a *karate chop*. They do this by striking at the bottle's weakest point: its outer curve.

I do not recommend breaking a bottle with a *shuto* because you will probably cut your hand with the broken edges of the bottle. There is very little pain involved in breaking a brick with your hand or cracking a tile with your head, though all of these have some danger of harm involved in doing them.

Many of these tricks and acts that I have described are dangerous techniques. Skilled performers demonstrate these acts and you should not be too surprised by them. Nor should you believe that they convey any real *budô* skill or mastery. It is very dangerous to do these if you are an amateur and, for this reason, they can be considered a form of art. You should not have contempt for these techniques, because they do take intelligence, and some of these tricks can be used to help you in a moment of need.

SIMILARITY BETWEEN BUDÔ PERFORMANCES AND DRAMA SCENES

Mass communication is thriving these days. Because of that, I have more opportunities to teach and supervise *budô* performances and stunts. I have done research and supervised such movies as ***Shinobi no Mono*** and **007**. The trend of *tate* [formal fighting scenes] has changed from tradition to realism and from realism to abstraction. It is not always easy to judge which is better. We must all understand that a *tate* performance must be made to fit a scene. The most formal of *tate* can be seen in *Kabuki*.

The *tate* in ***Ranpeimono kyo*** and ***Suzuga mori*** [popular *Kabuki*] are superb. Even in the stage performance, the producers studied and infused realism into the pivotal scenes by using real water or real blood. Since the release of ***Tateshi Danpei*** [sword fight acting instructor] and ***Sawa Sho*** [famous actor] there has been a tendency to emphasize realism in movies rather than formality. This came about after Danpei was struggling to figure out how to demonstrate realism for his audience. One day while pondering how to show realism in the movies, Danpei became intoxicated, and got beaten up in a fight. This story is a very famous one — how Danpei grasped essential meaning of realism through this fight. Without any doubt, it is very difficult to accomplish realism on stage. Enoken-*san* [comedian] is said to have used a real sword when he was acting as the character Kondo Isami for *tate*. That might be his attempt to accomplish realism, if only for his own feeling. The actors around him would also run away because they knew he was using a real sword, and that made the scene even funnier.

If you over-emphasize realism in a movie or such, this would make the *tate* boring. According to a story by Yumio Nawa [martial arts historian], there was a scene in **The History of Civil Punishment** involving the torture of a stripper. The actress was tied, nude and put among a few snakes where she was to act as if overcome with fear. Yet, she was not afraid of the snakes and therefore unable to perform her scene well. In order to put more realism into the scene, the crew released a barrel full of snakes and all hell broke loose. The actress then began crying and screaming, shaking desperately. This is going much too far.

After filming this scene, the directors thought it would look very real. However, when they reviewed the film, their expectations were dashed and they had to reshoot the scene. This story illustrates the role of proper producing.

I think an *enbu* [martial arts demonstration] should be adjusted according to the scene's plot or the environment. In a huge theater, the *enbu* should be performed slowly and in a relaxed way, and for the television, it should be brief and spirited. The movements in the performance can be shown in the style of a traditional slow dance [*mai*] or dramatization. In addition, it would be good to design the *enbu* and *tate* in natural body movements.

While an *enbu* is only a performance of *budô*, it must contain heart. The main issue is how to express this heart through technique. Let me explain the way I did an *enbu* at Japanese Budôkan. After the demonstration of *Jikishinei ryu*, we performed a demonstration of *Togakure ryu ninpô*. The demonstrators were five persons: Mariko Hatsumi, three of my senior students, and myself. All bowed towards the *kamiza* and then we turned to greet the people at the convention:

"Let me say a word to all before we begin. In America, there is a popular interest in the academic discipline of kinesiology — in other words, the study of body motion. There is also a way to communicate and understand intentions through gestures and motions. I hope you enjoy our demonstration, from which I adopted some of these ideas and techniques. *Hozutsu* get set!"

One student is holding the *hozutsu* [ninja cannon] in the center of the convention hall. "Ready. Aim," and then I give the signal to fire. He fires the cannon and white smoke emerges. (The audience is startled.)

"We will perform a demonstration of *taijutsu* next. This *taijutsu* is unique to our tradition." The moment when the *uke* [attacker, receiver] believes he has won by throwing off his *tori* [defender], the *tori* punches at the *uke.* Then the *tori* applies *kappo* [revival methods] to the *uke* as he was knocked unconscious. The *uke* is restored to consciousness.

Both the *tori* and *uke* leap at each other with *kiai.* They exchange punches and kicks, until the moment when the *uke* throws the *tori* with *seoi nage* [shoulder throw]. Both of the *tori*'s fists strike the *uke*'s ears. The *uke* falls over, holding his head. While the *tori* is in midair he readjusts his body to land on his feet.

The *tori* then helps the *uke* up, rubs the *uke*'s ears with hands, and gives *issui no katsu* [*see* **Expert Control To Revive Or Kill**]. The *uke* comes back to consciousness. (Audience applauds.)

<u>*Onikudaki Gaeshi*</u>

Both men exchange a few punches. The *uke* quickly grasps *tori*'s right hand in *oni gyaku* and tries to force him to surrender. The *tori* pretends to surrender, but then flips himself over and throws a punch into the *uke*'s solar plexus while landing. The *uke* falls to the ground and rolls away to the side. *Tori* applies *taikai no katsu* to the unconscious *uke*. Then the *uke* regains consciousness and stands up. (More applause.)

<u>*Sotogake gaeshi nadare*</u>

The *tori* and *uke* exchange punches and kicks until *uke* grabs his opponent's right hand and throws him with *nadare osotogake*. The *tori* turns himself in mid air and kicks *uke* in the groin as he lands. The *uke* hops a few times holding his groin and then falls down. The *tori* gives his partner *kin katsu* with his right leg while holding *uke* up from behind. The *uke* comes alive with a sigh. (Audience laughs.)

(The next demonstration is mine. This is *kappo* [*see* **Expert Control To Revive Or Kill**] using spiritual power. It may look like something mysterious yet comical, but I would like to show you that *kappo* is definitely possible through spiritual power.)

The *uke* grabs my lapel and tries to choke me. I tighten my neck muscles, raise my shoulders, and press my chin to my chest. This hinders the *uke* from choking me.

Then, in a flash, my hands grasp *uke*'s *butsumetsu* and I begin to squeeze them. The *uke* cannot stand the pain and throws both of his hands up in the air. I obstruct my opponent's eyesight by hitting into his face with my forehead. At the same time, I knee him in the groin. He releases me, staggers forward eight steps and falls down. I stand up and do both *kuji* and *kiai*. The *uke* comes alive and gets up. (Applause.)

The *uke* tries to punch me with his right fist. I strike up under his attacking forearm with my left fist. His right arm raises up, and then he attacks, punching me with his left fist. I kick up under his arm with my right foot. The *uke*'s left arm slides upward and trembles, but he tries to kick me with his left leg. I strike his leg away with my left fist and the *uke* collapses in pain. He manages to stand up, despite the pain, and grabs my lapel with his right hand. I attempt to apply *ganseki otoshi* on him, but as he resists, I launch a left *shuto* to his eyes. The *uke* throws his head backward and I torque his body. The *uke* soars away, twisting like a tornado. At that moment, I emit a piercing *kiai.* The *uke* falls backward again as if he is unconscious. After a few moments, I apply *kiai katsu* and he comes back to "life." (Applause.)

One *uke* makes *ittô no kamae* with a *katana* while his partner makes *tosui no kamae*. They move about me, trying to attack. Immediately, I throw *metsubushi* at them. Both men are blinded while I leap between them, strike into their vulnerable points, and roll away. I stand up in *kamae* and give *kiai katsu*. Both of my opponents stand up. (Applause.)

(The next demonstration displayed the usage of special ninja weapons. The first showed the use of *tekagi no jutsu*. The technique showed how to apply *shuko* to grasp the enemy's body or to catch an attacker's sword.)

Mesashi no jutsu

A ninja disguised as an old man walks toward the *uke* limping. The *uke* notices this man's attention and attacks him with a sword. The *tori* dodges the attacking sword using *taihenjutsu*. The *uke* prepares for another attack. The moment the *uke* sees his rival is defenseless, he makes the sword cut downward from *dai jodan*.

At that moment, the *uke*'s *tsue* [walking stick] opens to reveal a lance, which he stabs at the *tori*'s chest. The *uke* pulls his javelin and then tries to launch it at the *tori.* The *tori* knocks it upward with his *tsue*. The lance flies out of the *uke*'s hand. The *tori* sweeps the end of the *tsue* across the *uke*'s legs. The *uke* falls down. (The walking stick has a secret: there is lead inserted into the middle of this stick. This weighted-stick can be used to hit and break bones.) The *tori* finishes off *uke*, launching *kage no ippon* towards the *uke*'s skull. (Applause.)

[The next demonstration involved a four-foot five-inch *shinobi tsue*. This is a weapon made of a hollowed out bamboo with a chain in it.

Both ends have hooks and weights. The next demonstration involves a six-foot staff with a weighted-chain hidden inside.]

The *uke* does *ittô seigan kamae* [one-sword true-eyes posture]. The *tori* begins in *jodan no kamae* and tries to thrust his sword low under his *uke*'s *bô*. The *uke* leaps back and away to avoid the attack while the *tori* follows by immediately striking the *bô* downward. The hidden chain flies out and catches the *uke*'s sword. Then a tug-of-war game begins between them (the convention hall echoes with voices yelling, "Pull! Pull!"). The *tori* counts the timing of the push-pull rhythm, and moves forward to sweep his *bô* tip along the *uke*'s leg. The *uke* falls down onto his back. The *tori* thrusts his *bô* toward *uke* with perfect timing. (Applause.)

(In the next demonstrations, we presented a lesson in the *sanshaku bô* [*hanbô*]. The *tori* was Mariko Hatsumi. She then followed with a demonstration of a *kaiken* [waist dagger].)

Kaiken no kata - Ipponme

A sword-wielding attacker tries to cut the *kunoichi* Mariko; she throws a poison snake at him. Taken by surprise, the *uke* tries to kill the snake by cutting downward with his sword. Then the *uke* has lost his composure and tries to cut the *kunoichi*. She plunges the *kaiken* into her attacker's jugular vein while twisting her body away. The *kunoichi* then stabs *uke* in the heart.

Kaiken no kata - Nihonme

The *uke* tries to cut *tori* with *sutemi no kamae* while the *kunoichi* is shifting into *choka no kamae*. As she shifts around she releases *metsubushi* from her dagger sheath. At the moment in which the cloud of powder causes the *uke* to lose concentration, the *kunoichi* stabs his Adam's apple with her dagger.

(The next demonstration is called *bisento no jutsu*. The *bisento* is a very heavy weapon; a sword attached to the tip of a staff. With this weapon, warriors could easily cut through an enemy's armor or a horse's legs.)

The *uke* has a *katana* while the *tori* swings a *bisento* at him. (This demonstration reminds me of the fight between Benkei and Ushiwakamaru [young Minamoto no Yoshitsune].) The attacker's *taihenjutsu* is superb but the *bisento* makes a relentless cutting noise. It sounds like "*hyu hyu*." Ultimately, the *tori* cuts the *uke*'s legs with his blade point. The *uke* shows, through body language, that he has been wounded by the razor edge. Without hesitation, the *tori* swings the *bisento* down atop the *uke*'s head. (This is called *kabuto wari* [helmet breaker].)

(The next *enbu* displays the use of the *kyoketsu shoge* [hooked blade weapon with weighted cord]. This weapon is said to be an older version of the *kusarigama*. If you were unable to do these techniques, you would also be unable to master *shinobi nawa no jutsu*. *Kyoketsu shoge* means "running through mountains and fields." Let me explain this *enbu*. Masaaki Hatsumi is the *tori*.)

The *tori* begins in *hachiji buri* [figure-eight swing] and then changes to *yoko buri* [sideways swing]. The *tori* launches the weighted-end [*fundo*] toward the *uke*'s face. *Uke* avoids this attack, shifting his body. *Tori* retrieves the *fundo* preparing for another chance to attack. Then he uses the *fundo* to strike his *uke*'s hands. The *uke* drops his sword. Now, the *tori* swings the *fundo* at his opponent's feet several times to distract him. Suddenly, the *uke* catches the *fundo* while the *tori* seems to miss the feat. But, in fact, the *tori* is deceiving his partner. The *tori* removes a *shuriken* from his chest pocket and throws it at *uke*'s face. The *uke* clutches his wounded face. In that moment, the *tori* wraps the *uke*'s left hand with rope to bind him. Now, the *uke* has lost control of his left hand and tries to kick with his right leg. The *tori* strikes the attacker's leg (at a vulnerable point) with the *kyoketsu shoge*. The attacker falls down. The *tori* binds and throws *uke* with *gozen nage* by pulling the rope wrapped around the *uke*'s left hand. The *uke*'s body is dragged around with the rope. The *tori* cuts *uke*'s neck with the *shoge* [sickle]. (Applause.)

(The final performance is *sojutsu*. This demonstration is based upon a legend from ancient times when it was said that a spear should have a length greater than six feet. The *tori* is Masaaki Hatsumi.)

The *tori* begins by shifting the *yari* from *jodan* to *ihen no kamae.* The *uke* does *kamae* with his sword resting on his shoulder. The *tori* tries to thrust the *yari* into the *uke*'s chest. The *uke* takes a step backward as the *tori* kneels down and thrusts the *yari* upward under the swordsman's arms. The *uke* changes his body position to avoid the attack (*taijutsu itten*). Again, the *tori* jabs the *yari* towards the *uke*'s neck. The *uke* blocks the *yari* attacks with his sword. *Tori* leaps backward about two yards and then drives the *yari* point at the *uke.* The *uke* avoids this attack and makes *totoku no kamae* [shielding sword posture]. The *tori* takes a couple of steps back and tries thrusting attacks from both right and left sides. However, the *uke* has flawless *kamae* and blocks all attacks. The *tori* leaps backward and then makes *sutemi no kamae* with his spear tip returning to a low position. The *uke* makes *dai jodan no kamae* and both start to run at each other with powerful *kiai.* The *uke* throws his sword at his opponent, but the *tori* deflects it upward with his *yari.* Yet, the sword's tremendous momentum breaks the *yari* into two sections. (The bladed portion of the broken *yari* flies up to the *Budôkan*'s second row seats.) In a flash, the *tori* strikes down onto his attacker's head with the remaining piece of the *yari* [called *tsuka*].

The *enbu* ends. All members bow to the *kamiza*. The *Budôkan* fills with applause.

This demonstration succeeded in being different from the formalized *enbu* at the *Budôkan*. We need to change the way Japanese *kobudô* are performed or they will become outdated. It is time for all martial artists to reconsider the performances of *budô*. We must have a burning desire to revitalize our demonstrations and exhibitions so that they are appropriate for modern audiences. At the *Budôkan*, I kept checking the impressions of our audience while we did our *enbu*. Overall, the audience seemed to enjoy the *enbu*, applauding and laughing quite often. The *budô* specialists in attendance seemed to be intensely studying our movements. It is my belief that modern demonstrations should entertain the general populace and satisfy the curiosity of professional martial artists.

When [Ichikawa] Danjuro IX began a new era of *Kabuki* called "sosakuge kikatsureki." It was his intention to revitalize the history of *Kabuki*. My demonstration of martial arts, the *enbu* above, is my idea for a *katsubu enbu* [resuscitating martial arts exhibitions].

Incidentally, several days after we performed the *enbu* at the *Budôkan*, I was asked this question by one of my students:

"*Sensei,* during the *Budôkan* demonstration you performed with the *kyoketsu shoge*, at one point, the *fundo* ring came off, dropped in front of your opponent, and then you just stood without making any *kamae*. Were you startled by this accident or were you just baiting him?"

I answered him as follows, and unraveled his confusion. "As you guessed the ploy was intentional. A human being cannot be considered knowledgeable in the *budô* until he is able to exhibit *suki* [unguarded points] to his opponent. If you were to show *suki* to an amateur, they would view it as an enticement to attack, and would act against that area. At that moment, you could swiftly counterattack. Clearly, you cannot win unless you are perceptive enough to discern whether the *suki* is a genuine weakness or a deception. Ooishi Kuranosuke [leader of the 47 Ronin] showed *suki* by acting like he was a fool. When *saints* get down to work, they often become fools. After learning the important lessons of *fudôshin* [immovable spirit] and *suki* one can truly discover the unbeatable techniques of *sutemi* [self-abandonment]."

"In addition, if you perform the demonstration [*enbu*] perfectly with absolutely no flaws, the audience will get bored with the event. It is a good idea to show some mistakes here and there, intentionally. The audience will be thrilled to see how you deal with them. Without a doubt, I believe this will cause a connection or bonding between the audience and the performer."

EXPERT CONTROL TO REVIVE OR KILL: A WOUND NEED NOT BE FATAL

A person can be affected to live or die by physical stimulus, chemical stimulus, or spiritual stimulus. *Budôka* knock people down with an *atemi* [strike], then revive them with *kappo* [revival methods]. The places to apply *kappo* are called *kyusho* [nine places], *kyusho* [vulnerable points], and *kyusho* [incense burning points] according to various traditions. Nevertheless, what it represents is always the same.

Kyusho [nine places] does not signify the nine places to strike on an opponent's body. In the Japan of yesteryear, the number nine represented the apex or pinnacle of something. Therefore, the word indicated the most effective point upon a person's body to apply *kappo*. The actual number of *kyusho* is uncountable. Each individual martial art tradition had its own secret places to apply *kappo,* which it passed down to the succeeding generation. The areas of the body that provide intense sexual pleasure can be called *ikutokoro [iku = kyu* of *"kyusho,"* a pun since *iku* also implies "climax"].

Kyusho most probably referred to a point that could be lethal when struck. This *kyusho* is most likely derived from the word *keiraku* (meridian) or *keiretsu* (Chinese medical term). In the *denshô* of *Hontai Takagi Yoshin ryu jutaijutsu,* it states, "There is a cure called *dosui-katsu*. If you have a serious problem in the area of the *suigetsu,* put *kyu* [burning incense] on *kinketsu* [special places for curing]. There are *kinketsu* in the chest area, on the tailbone, and between the thumb and forefinger."

Thus, a human's *kyusho* have very important functions. They can be used as treatment points, to revive or extinguish someone. Let me introduce an interesting account of *toshin* [specific timing]: If you were hit upon the *kyusho* points called *kasumi, murasame,* or *kori* at midnight, you would die within a day. If you were hit upon the *tento, murasame, myojyo, goya,* or *kori* at 2 a.m., you would die after fourteen days. If you were hit upon the *tsukikage* or *toki noto* at 4 a.m., you would die after twenty days. If you were hit upon the *tento, myojyo,* or *hiji zume* at 2 p.m., you would die within a year's time.

In the Shorinji *hiden* [secret scrolls] it describes how to treat patients who were hit at critical times. There are vital points called *juniji ketsuro, nejiketsu zaitan, ushiji ketsuzaikan, toraju ketsuzaihai,* and *hitsuji jikeitsuzai shocho*. The explanations describe how to mix special medicines for these treatments. I often refer to my *denshô* of *toate* [concentrated attacks] because of how many patients I treat and how they all explain their chest ailments as having been caused by a blow received days earlier. Sometimes, it is as much as three days, seven days, fifteen days, or even thirty days before they come to me.

Let us move on to a story of *kappo:*

One day, Takamatsu *sensei* was walking along the riverside when he heard a woman's voice cry out, "My child fell into the river!" *Sensei* jumped into the river and managed to pull the child to safety. He immediately saw that the child had swallowed a lot of water. He knew it might not be too late to save this child and pulled on the child's lower lip with his fingers. It jerked back right away. This is one way that a *budôka* tests for life and death. If the unfortunate person's lower lip jerks back right away when pulled down, there is hope that this person will survive. *Sensei* then applied *suikatsu no katsu*, which made the child throw up water, and another *katsu* [resuscitation methods], called *taikai no katsu*, that helped the child breathe.

On another occasion, *Sensei* stood enjoying a wonderful sunset over a distant pond. Suddenly, he heard a young man leap into the water attempting suicide. *Sensei* leapt into the water, to rescue him. Though *sensei* tried *suishi no katsu* and *taikai no katsu* on the young man, he was without success.

Sensei told me, "When the child fell into the river he was trying hard to survive, he wanted to be saved. His spirit was vibrant. The young man, on the other hand, was determined to die. His spirit was dead before he ever entered the pond. That is why nothing I did would revive him." Here, we can all understand how important it is to have inner power and the will to live. You must have a strong spirit to live in times of illness and sickness. In time, the sickness will be forced to leave your body, pushed out by your will power.

What should you do if you are struck by a powerful *atemi*? There is a clever secret of how to cope with *atemi*. In the old days, there was *yobokappo* [preventive *kappo*]. This was a method to revive yourself, without help from anyone, when you were struck by *atemi*. First, sit in *seiza* with both arms at your sides. Push your hips backward as much as you can, straighten your spine, take a deep breath, and pronounce *"rin"* in your mind. While doing this, put your intention into your lower abdomen, tense your muscles, and then loosen them. Repeat these words nine times each: *pyo, to, sha, kai, jin, retsu, zai, zen*, and concentrate all of your energy in your abdomen. Next, put your intention in the calves of your legs, tensing and releasing, nine times. Continue by counting nine times as you clench your fists and relax them. Then concentrate on your chest and belly, tensing and releasing nine times. Consequently, you do *yobokappo* thirty-six times in total and finish by licking a pinch of salt. Thereupon, for the next four hours you are able to revive yourself without *katsu* applied by others.

There are attacks by chemical toxins [poisons, etc.] but there are also *kappo* to revive victims of these attacks. *Suisei, kitsuke, gusuri,* and *ganyaku* are *kappo* against poisons. When I treat my patients, I make use of these remedies. For example, there is a *mumyo no katsu* [darkness point]. When you are poisoned by *torikabuto* [poisonous plant] or struck by *ganzen* [chemical], you warm your waist with roasted salt and hot ashes. You can treat the affliction by applying this as a cure. This same principle exists in *harimasui* [numbing pain through acupuncture].

You can give spiritual stimulation by chanting *jumon* [incantations] like *kuji* or *juji* [*see* **Endure Using Kuji**]. *Kappo,* likewise, practice *kassatsu jizai* [control over life and death] with *kiai* and chanting *kuji juji jumon.*

The Samurai are said to have saved people lives, revived themselves and regained composure because they knew three methods of *kassatsu jizai.* When a samurai told a wounded friend, "Your wound is not very deep," he was not just mouthing words, but using vocalized methods of revival that promoted inner strength. There has been a recent emergence of a neurological disease called *gendai byo* [contemporary illness]. I expect that this *kappo* can be used to cure these patients, who do not need medical treatment.

When I appeared on the television program called **Ninpô Stamina Cuisine,** I demonstrated ninja food such as the mountain potato, wild boar, frog, snake, and mouse. To my surprise, I overheard a young actress on the show whispering, "Ninja were so cruel; they killed creatures without mercy." Even my students covered their ears when I killed a mouse.

After the show, I told my students: "I killed a mouse today but it was not a bad thing to do. I also hate to kill a living thing, but human beings have to be able to kill when it is necessary. In turn, after you take the life of any living thing, you must do ten good things. This is called *issatsu juzen*. If you only have sympathy for little creatures and close your eyes to more important issues, you are not worthy to live in a society of all living creatures. Have any of you heard the story of the monk that killed a cat to save his disciples?"

This is a story about monks in training. They were having an argument about whether or not a particular cat had the qualities of Buddha. The Zen priest Nanzen Osho had been absent from the debate but entered to hear the monks arguing. When he noticed the mood in the temple, he picked up the cat and held it. "Say something; say one thing. If any of you speaks, this cat will live. Or, I will kill it." None of the monks said a word.

"You people were arguing about it continually. Now, you cannot say a thing, can you?" Then he cut the cat in half. He asked Joshu [one of his disciples], "What do you think of my killing this cat?" Joshu silently put his straw sandals on his head and walked away. He showed total acquiescence to Nanzen Osho.

Thus, even a Zen high priest did what was necessary when the time came for taking a life — and saved the spiritual lives of his students.

DEVELOPMENT OF BATTLEFIELD METHODS EMPHASIZING REGIONAL TRAITS

Kakuto jutsu [battlefield methods] differs depending upon the climate of the place and the natural trait of the people. In Chinese *kenpô* [fist way], northern *kenpô* and southern *kenpô* are different in character. Northern *kenpô* in general is aggressive, because northern people are generally poor and scant in clothing, food, and housing. On the contrary, southern peoples' *kenpô* tends to counterattack the enemy (they attack after avoiding the enemy's attack first), because they are blessed with nature's abundance.

Generally speaking, karate is believed to be developed by Okinawan people using hand chops and kicks, which were invented because they were disarmed by the lord of Shimazu. One of Okinawa's scholars explains, "I think the origin of karate was influenced by ancient China. People in Okinawa, in each village, passed down this technique in secret. The people who used this *kenpô* rearranged the moves and it became karate. Not everybody in the village learned karate, but a few did. The person who was called master did practice without drinking *sake* [rice wine]. They used to demonstrate the karate dance at festivals and special occasions. As far as I saw, old karate was more flexible than today's karate, which seems rigid. There seemed to be a big difference between old karate and karate after World War II. As you know, a big country has ruled Okinawa. They tend not to show their characters or emotions on their faces. Okinawa's gestures are comparatively small to the people in Honshu, and they do not like to express emotions such as happiness, anger, grief, or joy."

Therefore, you may see their punch as a kind of explosion that comes out of their repressed anxiety.

Nomads were good at horse riding, bow and arrow, and swordwork. People in ancient China were good at *shuriken* and *naginata,* while the clans that lived in the mountains were good with a hatchet. Pygmy tribes kill beasts with a lethal blowgun and catch fish with javelins.

Like these above, innumerable tribes fight with weapons that normally are used to catch food. In addition, depending upon the trait of the land or religion, their principle of fighting differs based on their way of examination and way of thinking. What kind of land grows people who are good at war? The first to come to my mind is a country where people endure and keep things in order in a simple way. In the Japanese army, the people from Kyushu and Tohoku were said to be the strongest.

Minamoto Yoritomo cherished a simple way of life, maintaining the principles of thriftiness and strength. This character trait can make a person strong. There is nothing more fragile than a culture that indulges in lavishness. The Fujiwara and Heike clans are good examples of strength and lavishness.

Contemporary Japanese people cannot be careless about their lifestyles either. They are proud of economic growth and praise themselves for being a cultural nation. On the other hand, people are losing both physical and mental strength, they are plagued with physical and mental maladies, and they create public hazards everywhere. When people pursue a cultural lifestyle only, and forget the natural slow-paced lifestyle, their humanistic sentimental reflection gets dull, and they slowly lose their vitality.

At the time of the Meiji period's exploding cultural development, they dropped the necessity of learning fighting methods and *kobudô* [ancient martial arts], and encouraged the changing style of *budô* into a sports form. I think that kind of change is fine, but I cannot explain how sad I feel for those people who are striving to become real *budô* masters.

NAGE: NOT ONLY FROM THE LOINS

A famous doctor for the hip and waist, Dr. Shioya, said, "If a person has a good waist and hips [loins], he will be healthy and smart too, professional baseball players and sumo wrestlers especially must take good care of their waist and hips. Asahio retired because of injuries to his waist and hips. The baseball pitcher Kaneda hurt his hip and waist and could not play well for quite a while. The baseball player should not play Mah Jong before he enters the ballpark. The waist and hips' muscles and bones sustain a person's torso. Mah Jong makes them bend forward and get tired. One of the reasons the sumo sect that played maj jong all the time never did well was because of this. When the body gets tired it shows on the waist and hips."

It is true that hips are an essential part of the body. Because of this notion, people believe *nagewaza* [throwing techniques] in general are believed to work from the hips. However, it is not that simple.

The *nagewaza* of judo is sorted out as *tewaza* [hand techniques], *koshiwaza* [hip techniques], *ashiwaza* [leg techniques], *masutemiwaza* [sacrifice techniques], and *yokosutemiwaza* [side sacrifice techniques]. The arm power of *tewaza* and leg power of *ashiwaza* tend to be an advantage foreigners have over the Japanese.

Japanese could be world class players if *waza* was limited to *koshi* [loins] only, but they cannot be optimistic judging from *tewaza* and *ashiwaza*. Therefore, *nage* lies in the whole body.

However, we cannot ignore the important function of *koshi*. *Koshi* holds and protects the guts. In addition, if you compare guts with plants, guts would be like roots, and a big tree with wide roots underground never sways even in a bitter wind. The root sucks up nutrients from the soil. The human takes nutrients through the guts.

One day, Takamatsu *sensei* gave me a *haramaki* [scarf for wearing around the belly]. I was deeply moved by his attentive consideration for my keeping my belly warm. The roots underground are constantly protected with the temperature of the soil.

Now, there is a method to strengthen ninjas' legs and lower body. It is to run over bumpy roads holding about four pails full of water over the shoulders with a long *bô*. This method is important for building up strength, holding weight over the lower body and teaching the body the rhythm at the same time. Old age shows from the legs and lower body first. *Bujin* always take good care of their legs and lower body. However, they should not be cowardly or fearful of every small misfortune.

In addition, the loins are closely related to reproduction. It is useless to try to build up sexual endurance by giving stimulus only to the genitals. You have to know the health of the whole body and the balance of hormones. In other words, the harmony of mind, technique, and body [*shin-gi-tai*] is the key to endurance in matters of love.

TRAIN YOUR MENTAL ENERGY

Your physical motor ability is considered both kinematic [physical] and spiritual [mental]. Generally, "motor" means the former while the latter tends to be considered less significant.

Once upon a time, there was a sword master who was famous for being the best in the *dojo* with the wooden sword, but when he held a real sword, his mind froze with fear and he lost his concentration completely. As this example shows, the person who has weak willpower makes his body weak also.

Therefore, *bugeisha* trained their capacity for focus and willpower by learning Zen. Zen's questions and answers might have been a kind of method to develop these mental abilities.

The most effective way to train the mind is unquestionably *keiko* [training or practice]. Like a cook cannot know the taste of his food without eating it, *budôka* cannot know the taste of *budô* without *keiko*. The best thing is to go to the *dojo* and devote yourself to *keiko*. In addition, in daily life, you have to remember to calm your mind by listening to music and doing good things that feed your mind with positive energy.

This is how to develop a strong, flexible spiritual ability.

Another important thing is to eat natural foods, not food that makes your blood acidic. When you get acidosis, you are easily provoked and lose your perseverance. Liver problems, abnormal blood pressure, and neurotic trouble also can erode your mental-motor ability.

If a person who loves to drink, be violent at home, or chase women all the time and make trouble, were to develop the mental abilities that I have described, he could quit drinking *sake*, stay away from women, and conquer the pain of desires.

I accomplished mental control by developing my mind and motor ability through *budô*. The most important thing is to learn physically first, then understand the theory. The only way to accomplish this is to do *keiko*. I learned much from my *sensei* and listened to good lectures, but it was much later, after three or five years of constant *keiko*, and training to digest these experiences, that I really absorbed them in my mind. The philosophy of *budô* is only a process for *budôka* to understand that the taste of this philosophy can only be taken in through the mouth of *keiko*.

CUT AND GET CUT

In *kenpô* [sword way], there is a training method called *tameshi giri* [test cut]. Sometimes the trainee cuts a person or a bunch of straw. In karate, they have *tameshi wari*, to break a pile of tiles.

If you think this is the ultimate technique of cutting or breaking, you are a total novice in the world of *budô*, because this is only one of the many ways to cut in *budô*.

The other day I asked one of my *deshi* [disciples]: "Now do you understand the song in my ***Bôjutsu*** book, that when you thrust the *bô* in the air, you feel something?"

And my *deshi* answered: "That means you can start feeling something when you keep practicing with the *bô*, thrusting it in the air, doesn't it?"

Then I answered: "That actually means you should keep practicing until you find there is nothing in the air, no matter how many times you thrust the *bô* hard in the air." So many students make such a simple answer meaninglessly difficult.

On the day of *taijutsu* training, I let the *deshi* do the *keiko* of *senbon musha dori* ["thousand warrior catch"]. Everybody was doing this *keiko* correctly, even the beginner students. In the meantime, when they got tired, some started to cut corners. Then I gave them *kiai*. After most of them gave up (long before reaching a thousand) my only foreign student was still doing *keiko*, not showing any tiredness at all. He did not become tired because he was doing *keiko* properly without excessive power since he had dislocated his elbow during an earlier lesson.

This example shows you that *keiko* will be totally ineffective when you try too hard to cut or to win. Therefore, you end up not getting the knack of *keiko*. Once you have acquired this knack, you do not have to do *keiko* a thousand times.

In addition, when you are preoccupied with the act of cutting, like cutting firewood, you cannot develop as *budôka* at all. I once heard

Takamatsu *sensei* say that when his *deshi* Akimoto died, "I wish I could have died instead of him."

This indicates that a warrior should have the inclination to be cut instead of cutting others. Therefore, every negative feeling, hatred, or regret should be cleared from your mind. Once you gain the willingness to be cut, you can understand a phrase like "put up with shame and put away vengeance" easily. This relates to feeding other people even when you are hungry, the feeling of *hara-kiri* [play on words between suicide for the sake of saving lives and giving up food when you are hungry].

Man should live with a willingness to be cut. He will naturally become a vital person in society and will learn to live more happily by winning without drawing the sword, cutting, or killing people.

Some friend told me that I have a strong tendency to become a religious person. I answered: "It goes without saying I have that quality in me. We have a law called *jin bujin fusatsu no ho* [god and warriors never kill except when unavoidable]. That is because we gain the mind of *shumon* [religion] through mastering *budô*. We are supposed to tend this religious nature with *budô*."

FOOTWORK REVEALS YOUR MIND AND BODY

It has been written in the ***Shoniki*** (ancient ninja text) that there are ten ways of walking known collectively as the *Ashinami Jukkajo.* They are:

Nuki Ashi	silent step
Suri Ashi	short, sliding step
Shime Ashi	constricting step
Tobi Ashi	short leaping step
Kata Ashi	single leg step
O Ashi	long stride step
Ko Ashi	short stride step
Kizami Ashi	cutting step
Wari Ashi	feet pointed in opposing directions
Tsune No Ashi	ordinary walking

However, the most basic step to master is the technique of walking upon ice with *geta* [wooden clogs]. One who masters this method of walking has good control of one's center of gravity and thus, is very stable. Therefore, one can easily clear any obstacles while walking. With this step, one feels as if his body is floating in the air.

Once when I was visiting Takamatsu *sensei* at his home, Mr. Akimoto who was an instructor and one of his best students, entered the house and walked up the stairs to the second floor without making a sound. I truly admired his footwork.

Eiji Yoshikawa wrote about the footwork of a *budô* master in his book: ***Yagyu Sekishusai***. When I read it, I was surprised to find out that it was the same as what Takamatsu *sensei* had taught me.

It was a terribly cold December day and the powdery snow from the border mountains of Iga was falling continuously. The wooden floor of the outside corridor was frozen like a mirror and was constantly covered by the snow even if one had just wiped it clean. The people around Sekisensai were nervous whenever he walked down the corridor, but he never slipped.

"Why?" someone asked doubtfully; "he is sick and so weak." Sekishusai answered him with a slight smile like a withered leaf. "When I walked down the frozen floor, I invented the Ukimi no Ho (floating step). It can also be called the Ukimi no Tachi (floating sword). I will teach this to Masakimi and Hyogo..."

Several days later, he passed away at the mature age of 78. It was a silent day in the Yagyu valley, which was completely covered by snow. His calm death reflects his great life. Sekishusai might have known that he was about to die, but he continued to train and improve his kenjutsu. He was even practicing his strikes with a bokken in the corridor until a few days before he died. He should be called a true master. (Quoted from ***Yagyu Sekishusai***)

When you have mastered this type of walking, you will know that it is the most essential footwork. There is a special footwork that is based upon walking upon a frozen floor or ice and it is this type of movement that one should learn in order to master ninjutsu.

Although many people think of *yoko aruki* (sideways walking) as a unique walking step in ninjutsu, the philosophy behind the walking methods are more important. These are: *Eyes of legs*, *Ears of legs*, *Nose of legs*, and the *Touch of legs*.

Eyes of legs means the ability to judge if one can move or walk without making noise.

Ears of legs is the ability to judge your opponent's footwork, to change the sound of your steps by the use of special footwear, or even hiding your own footprints so that you cannot be followed.

Nose of legs is to control one's odor. Putting a "smell bag" on the floor to hide one's scent is an example of this technique. Another example is to use a female dog if a male dog is being used to track you.

Touch of the legs means walking carefully, as if one is walking on air, so that should one step on an object such as *tetsubishi* [caltrops], one can escape without injury.

Although there are many other considerations such as judging one's distance, your mental attitude is very important.

The legs of the *bugeisha* must be kept healthy. First of all, it is important to keep your legs warm at all times. Always wear socks, even during the summer. Secondly, one should walk for at least one hour each day.

You should also exercise your big toes by rotating them ninety times a day. This is an exercise to keep your liver and pancreas in good health. This is also said to be effective for women's beauty and men's sexual potency. Another good exercise for the legs is to push into the sole of your foot with your thumb. This helps stabilize one's blood pressure and is good for mental health. Now, with all that we have discussed and with what has been explained, you should be able to employ these methods as well as learn from other people's employment of them.

CHAPTER THREE

LIFE OF PERSEVERANCE

PEOPLE WHO CANNOT BEAR LIFE DO NOT LIVE

This is an age of crazy price fluctuations. People have fallen head over heels into the mire of inflation because of the surging economy called "*Jinmu Keiki*." Many people are in despair and losing direction, are they not?

I have no desire to dwell upon these people or sympathize with them. I think there is a wonderful opportunity to develop your life in spite of these circumstances, by making the best use of *shinobi* [perseverance]. We have to reflect upon this age of "the disposable," while we enjoy such material abundance.

Originally, the country of Japan did not have much in the way of material goods. It is a natural result considering its small land size and huge population. Moreover, our modern population explosion is a worldwide phenomenon. At world conferences on population, food shortage crises and population policy are discussed as international themes.

People are living in discomfort. However, the ninja had no problem within these conditions. If they do not have a large amount of material goods, they manage to live with a fresh approach to life. Furthermore, if people give up pursuing material goods they can return to a more humanistic society. In fact, I am rather glad to see the current world situation becoming chaotic. By the way, what guidelines do ninja use to live?

If you were cut upon one limb, you could still act by using your other limbs. Likewise, people have to use substitutes for economic power. Since Japan's economic power is weak in material goods, we should strengthen our technical and mental economic powers to better cope.

Surrounded by the sea, Japan can make "*suiton*" [water evasion] an economic resource. The sun shines upon every country, so if we should lose energy we might invent a device such as a solar energy condenser "*nitton*" [sun evasion] and reserve energy by "*futon*" [wind evasion] with windmills. Thus, there are innumerable ways to survive by *shinobi*'s techniques.

It may sound crude, but if we do not have fire, we have to go to bed early, wake up early, and eat uncooked foods. There seems to be a preference for natural foods that is quietly spreading. It is good for your health to eat uncooked foods. Take off your clothes when it is hot and put on more clothes when it is cold. Such simple strategies help us survive. Remember the children's verse:

Don't be so proud to be a human being.
Yo-i, yo-i.
A bear can sleep without heat made from oil.
Yo-i, yo-i.
De Kan Sho (chorus)

People who are proud to be cultured and learned, and act like nobility are nevertheless the first to fuss over a mere oil shortage. How impatient these noblemen are! Is this real human nature? Isn't this the time to make an effort to endure hardships?

ENDURE USING KUJI

Some people think a ninja can make a mystical *kuji* sign with their fingers and vanish while chanting, "Doron, doron." I have no intention to criticize these people and salute their choice. *Kuji* is such a beneficial thing that it can liberate others and yourself simply by the intonation of a charm.

One night my wife complained that she could not get to sleep because of a toothache. I would have given her aspirin but I could not because she is allergic to it. I could not call a doctor because it was the middle of the night. So I applied a chant of calming and a charm of sleep; she went to sleep after twenty minutes. I told this story to Takamatsu *sensei* the next day. He said, "The wife always puts down the husband no matter how great he is, so it is fortunate that your spell works on her."

How can you master the essence of *jumon ketsu-in kuji*? The first step is to practice mentally, concentrating upon one thing; this is a training to focus your spirit. However, getting into mystical occultism is not healthy. You have to mix understanding with mysticism and avoid a discrepancy between your will and your actions, even for a split second. It is very difficult to devote yourself toward your purpose. It is understood that you should not lose your sincerity under these conditions. You have to cast your true heart without a wicked thought.

In other words, stop your breathing for a moment when you focus on your purpose; your hands, legs, and eyes will follow. This is one of the ways to master the *kuji* method. It is to strengthen your own spiritual power. Once you master this, you can overcome any kind of hardship.

I may simplify this method as, "pulling hard for my dear father" [a chant or song to encourage you to work harder; to work hard for somebody for whom you care]. It is to verbalize the effort for somebody else.

MAKE YOURSELF INVISIBLE

At some time, all of us wish we could become invisible. Hiding ourselves from other people's eyes makes us feel like we have gained perfect freedom. However, the human beings have six senses [*rokkan*]. Therefore, you cannot say you are invisible just because no one can see you.

As I mentioned in the second chapter, the ninja concealed themselves using various means and methods. But for modern people, "vanishing" means getting away from the filth of society or from the systems that bind them. They try to release themselves from the frustrations of daily life through drunkenness, gambling or sexual indulgence. You could also call these "vanishing." The aim is to make the mind transparent, not the body.

On the other hand, some types of people just rush recklessly at life. It is a desperate deed to destroy one's life with violent passions. It is a poor way to become invisible, from the ninja's point of view. *Shinobi no waza* [the ninja's enduring method] requires you to vanish without throwing your existence away.

To vanish is not to run away. On the contrary, it is to study society. If you become invisible, you can see other people better. It is not to disappear for wrongdoing. Rather it is important to live well while you make yourself vanish; this is the true assignment for a ninja.

GET RID OF YOUR INFERIORITY COMPLEX

Every human being has secrets. This is called "the subconscious mind" from a psychological perspective. This comes out as a pattern of individual action. Freud considered such behavior to be rooted in sexuality.

I tend to call it "as the boy, so the man." For example, if the child grows up starving in poverty, the experience remains in his mind throughout his life, just like a burn scar stays on the skin for a lifetime. It is said that only after you have fully eaten are you starved for sex. Then when you have passed your sexual prime, you will become very materialistic and desire notoriety.

By the way, when you meet someone who has a bigger secret than yours, sometimes you feel small and you withdraw, but other times it ignites your enthusiasm to strive. When you hear the words "inferiority complex," you tend to think of it as a sloppy, weak sentiment that losers possess. However, I think this is a lopsided view and a bit prejudiced; actually the inferiority complex can be a source for indispensable energy and personal motivation to build a castle around yourself so you can withstand attack.

If you look at the inferiority complex this way, ancient *budô* was a battle between individual secrets. In the *bushi*'s society, one was not supposed to show one's emotions. Therefore, *kuden* [oral teachings], *hikan* [secret scrolls], and *hiden* [secret teachings] were very attractive things for practitioners of the martial arts. However, if you openly showed your desire for these, you would be killed instantly by an attack.

Even now, in modern society, the person who clearly wants to make a mark in society will not make it. Sometimes we meet people who nonchalantly brag about their path to the top. That kind of person has already neutralized or lost their secret perspective.

To live with one's hidden spirit means to keep striving for life itself, and this can be called hope. The source of "making a mark in society" is in the hidden spirit (heart).

Therefore, the most important first step is to live confidently with your own hidden heart. By doing so, you can get rid of the inferiority complex. [The feeling of being a "loser."]

People often ask me what is my favorite technique [*waza*]. I always answer that I do not have one. This is because, for a practitioner of the martial arts, having a favorite *waza* tends to be fatal. It is the same as if a baseball player or boxer, having his "favorite technique" studied by a rival, finds himself facing certain defeat. Therefore, the loser would be the winner and the winner would be a loser [inferiority complex]. I think it is great to hear my students say that they cannot read my mind. I would like to say that any player who brags about his favorite technique should be considered a novice martial artist.

DO NOT FORGET HUMANITY

I want you to understand the reason why the TV period drama ***Kogarashi Monjiro*** became so popular. [The actor Atsuo Nakamura plays the Monjiro character.]

We are too busy to care for others in this modern society. The only person you can rely upon is yourself. I believe I emphasized this point earlier. I do not think it is good to depend upon someone, but it would be ideal to have others depend upon you. However, if you decide to ignore everyone else, trusting only yourself, you will soon become one of the busiest of all modern men. These days, currently called the "irresponsible times," began through such dull people gathering.

"It doesn't concern me," is one famous Monjiro quotes that best represents today's "irresponsible times." In reality, Monjiro never left without helping somebody. While he says, "It doesn't concern me," he still becomes involved and fights the villain. This is what is so very charming about the Monjiro character. He does justice to people's morality.

To give a helping hand to poor people and to want to save them is the humanity of Japanese, and of a warrior's heart. However, modern Japanese have forgotten this morality. I think that is why they feel discomfort when they see Monjiro — it shows that they really want to do the same. This must be the reason the Monjiro series gained such popularity.

I think that modern Japanese should express more of this Japanese morality. Too many people willingly hide their morality according to today's trends. You can be seen as an irresponsible person on the surface. If you find it easier to live that way, it is also a way of practice. You might be living in a nihilistic manner with a callous attitude but I would prefer you have the Japanese spirit deep in your heart. Compassionate people make others feel gracious and trustworthy.

In today's Japan, it is as if "we exist, and therefore the island of Japan exists." I think it should be reversed. People should remember that Japan is a small island with innumerable people living on it. Keeping this in mind say, "It doesn't concern me." Otherwise, Japanese who live on such a tiny island will not survive.

LEARN LESSONS THROUGH YOUR BODY

My theory is that to become a master of *budô* you must learn both literature and the martial arts. *Budô* skills should be gained through awareness and physical training. Things you have learned intellectually tend to be expressed in the past tense. On the other hand, if you learn by means of body awareness, you become keen on social changes and foresee the changes of the future.

A merchant in Osaka starts as an apprentice and goes through hard training with the notion that money means more than people do. Young beginning apprentices are thoroughly taught that if you cannot make money you cannot survive as a merchant. Under the class system based upon wealth, only those who can sense the future with their skin can grow and become successful. In other words, after they are trained to the bones in the way of the merchant and become full-fledged merchants, they can keep up with the social changes. Their accuracy can match that of college-educated economists.

The strength acquired in day-to-day life can be found in [Charlie] Chaplin's life. He was born into a poor family. One Christmas night his mother ordered him to get a bowl, so he could collect charity food. He did not have shoes, but his mother kept pestering and hurrying him to go. He wore shoes with holes and went out crying. Such experiences made his comedy profound. This experience allowed him to create the shoe-eating scene in **The Gold Rush** [1925] and a futuristic one in **Modern Times** [1936].

"Yotsuya Akasaka, Koji-Machi, the water flowing ... cats are full of fur and full of ashes," [comical tune] is a famous line of Atsumi Kiyoshi who portrayed ***Tora-san***. [This movie series has 49 episodes in which the main character meddles in other people's lives.] Even this actor, so comical and humorous, thought about suicide while he was ill in a hospital. Then he overcame his period of desperation. This why he became the character Tora and made his comedy full of poetry that crystallized through his awareness of death. And this is why people watch and love it. His acting abilities developed from his experiences.

If you are living with your mind focused on a daily routine, in spite of what you believe you are being shaped into a mold and will become rigid. Eventually you crumble with surprising frailty. '*Bunbu ryodo*' means to learn through literature and physical training. I would like to emphasize the importance of physical learning, because the mind is only a part of the whole body.

BE INDIFFERENT TOWARD GOSSIP

Gossip is bothersome and annoying. However, if such things bother you, you will always be far from mastering *budô*. Takamatsu *sensei* often heard gossip about his students. Every time he said, "*Budô* is not a technique. It is heart. If you do not have the right spiritual attitude, you have zero quality as a *budô* student. Gossips are purposeless men." In addition, he added, "If you have a complaint about somebody, say it to that person directly." He hated and condemned those who gossiped.

I saw ***Onna Tobakushi*** [The Female Gambler] on television the other day. There was a scene where the skilled gambler died before he could teach the female gambler the essence of "*tohonbiki*" ["measured true defeat"]. Before he died, the skilled gambler told her, "Act intimidated, repeat this mantra, and be bold." These words resolve most subtleties.

In other words, forget everything on your mind, do not hesitate under any kind of situation, you do not have to worry about anything if you have confidence in everything you do. These words are to be remembered in the business world. I have heard that in the business world review and dismissal by one's seniors has a great impact upon your future, but if you falter or surrender, you will not have a good life.

For instance, if your rival in the company received an invitation to go for a drink after work from your mutual boss, you cannot help but become a bit nervous about their meeting. You get restless thinking you must do something to get yourself invited.

If you have confidence, you should not care what they do. You must become *fudôshin* [immovable spirit]. It might be a very difficult thing to do but you cannot grow as a human if other people's words or actions constantly affect your mind.

A good superior keeps watching his men without saying anything. A company that cannot see the truly good workers and promotes brown-nosers will soon go bankrupt. If you think poverty is bad then you have to work diligently without being bothered by gossips.

CHANGE RATHER THAN PROGRESS

People today seem like they want to progress. It seems that the quicker and greater the progress, the better. However, academic progress, life's progress, scientific progress... don't all these lead to ruin? My theory may sound extreme.

What I really would like to say is that if we accomplish huge progress in a short time, we may lose a lot of life's essence and our lives may become tedious. In other words, progress in those fields does not enhance life very much.

On the other hand, we cannot stay at the same level, which would also be meaningless. Then what can we do? It is easy. We can just change our lives. It may not be progressing but transforming. Anyway, if we change, it will have an impact upon our environment. We had best begin to think this way.

To live with the fixed notion that we must constantly progress is a very shallow way of living. In order to enjoy and savor our lives, sometimes we should forget about progress, take a rest, and look for a change. People say our lives are enhanced by progress, and that times are good, but to tell the truth, we have only become lethargic.

Moreover, the foundation of the *budô* world is *henka* [variation] and *kyojitsu tenkan* [alternating reality and illusion]. The application of technique and the ability for appropriate change is more appreciated than split second techniques to defeat an enemy. Fast techniques may look dynamic and magnificent, yet just like having a short temper means losing control, they could be the cause of your self-destruction. If you flow with the fight, being flexible to the opponent's attack and changing your position, you will never be defeated.

Plainly, a technique using speed is only an intellectual way to defeat the enemy, while change is the natural *kamae* of blending and harmony. Today, there is no need to live through overthinking. I absolutely believe we should live naturally.

The word progress has a strong connotation meaning advancement. Therefore, a person caught up in these ideas expects to push forward, be in front, no matter how big and strong his enemy. Except, in battle, our enemy may fall forward. At this point, it would be great to shift our bodies to the side. This is why I feel it more appropriate to recommend the techniques of *henka* instead of those relying upon speed.

DO NOT DESIRE JEWELRY

Blinded by the wealth of a diamond, Omiya married into the house of Tomiyama. However, happiness eluded Omiya as she ended up living in misery because nothing was more important to her than the diamond. After my *sensei* died, I visited his house in hopes of retrieving his books. His wife and daughter told me they had burned them because mice had made a mess on them. I loathed those mice for a moment until then I remembered *sensei*'s words:

"Hatsumi-*kun*, don't desire jewelry all the time." I blushed. Man is not dignified while he desires treasures. He should be able to seek and make the treasures.

When I spoke to Mr. Toko Kon [Japanese author], he was writing a book called ***Aoki Ezochi*** [Blue Land of Edo]. I asked him, "Are there any Abe or Kiyohara regional literature remaining?" He said, "War is a terrible thing. I sought for a long time but it seems that they have all been destroyed." The worth of treasure is only to be evaluated by the person who seeks it. The treasure itself is not very important.

When I had a ninja exhibit at a department store, two ninja swords were stolen. The people who secured the exhibit area were afraid I would cut them with my other sword. They thought that because the sword is said to be the soul of the *bushi* that they needed to come to me to beg forgiveness. I told them, "I do regret that the swords were stolen. However, I was worried about how sorry you would feel for what happened and that you might become distressed. Of course, the sword is a treasure for the *bushi*, but if you get upset for losing it or if you cling to it too tightly, you cannot be called a real warrior. Please do not worry any more." Consequently, I saved them from further worry, suffering, and anxiety.

Since I do not have any children, there are some people worried about my successor. They feel it is a shame not having a person who succeeds me in all these skills. I appreciate their concern, but since I am just shining my heart by doing *budô*, I cannot regret if my *budô* passes with me.

TURN THREE POISONS INTO THREE MEDICINES

I usually think there are three poisons, which are drinking, gambling, and prostitution. Develop into a strong man; be free from *sake,* women, and money — that is my motto. Some people say, "If you really press that point, doesn't it mean the person is strange?"

They are saying that we, as humans, need the world of entertainment for curing the ailments of the business world. Of course, this is true. I am not so foolish as to deny it. However, you **can** make such a statement once you learn to turn three poisons into three medicines.

I describe them as three poisons because each one has an uncanny attraction for man. In fact, I know many cases where even a strong man degenerated when he became caught up with one of these poisons. Therefore, I believe they are nothing but poison for the man in *budô*, who is trying to live his life unreservedly for training.

However, these three should not be considered as poisons forever. If they were, life would become suffocating and lifeless. You need to consider them as poisons and never even look at them for a certain period, but when you have passed that period, you must become a person who can control them as three medicines. If you constantly consider them as poisons and live that way forever, you may become a maladjusted person.

Since each man has his own way of using them, however, it is very hard to suggest specific ways. After all, you have to judge for yourself, knowing your own character. Therefore, there is a danger in indulging in them but you had better approach them expecting 60 percent satisfaction and pleasure. If you stop drinking *sake* after sixty percent of your capacity, you should never fall into unconsciousness.

There is a saying: "the hero loves women." It is better to have one woman around than to have no woman at all. Although gambling can be a monster to destroy your mind, if you can control it as a pleasure you will be a master.

In ninjutsu, there is an admonition: it is OK to have three pleasures, but you could be poisoned to death by three pains caused by the three pleasures. In the writings of the ninja, a good drinking habit is called *"jogo,"* handling women well is called "*gego*," and mastering gambling is called "*mugo*."

LIVE YOUR EVERYDAY LIFE WITH THE MIND OF SUTEMI

In the world of *budô* there is a word and faith called *"sutemi"* [sacrifice]. There might be some people who view this word negatively and call it something like "willing to throw your life away" or "suicide," but that is not what it is.

Every human has a desire to live. However, no matter how you wish to live, when fate comes down on you, you cannot live anymore; that is reality. In the world of *budô,* we translate this fact as *shizen gensho,* "natural phenomenon," and we must not try to make our mind rigid by it or eliminate hesitation.

Modern men should have the same readiness for death, considering the various causes like cancer, traffic accidents, and incurable diseases. When you face death, it is too late to regret not doing things that you really wanted to do. Even if you try to pass on your wishes to somebody else, you may not be able to pass on your desire.

Some people may say it is a good idea to write a farewell letter. Yet I think if you live your daily life with the readiness of *sutemi,* there is no need to leave a farewell letter. According to the late Kawabata Yosunari's farewell letter, "Silent death is an infinite word." I think that is quite true.

A great artist finds joy devoting his life to his work. In a trance, he forgets the self while pouring himself into his work and finds an eternal life there. Not only the artist, but we too must live our lives that way.

In order to do so, we must have a clear purpose in our daily life. If we live our daily lives with *sutemi,* the mind of *budô*, and the passion of an artist who pours his soul into his works, we can almost forget about death, and never regret our life at the moment of its end.

It is almost a kind of ritual to leave a farewell letter. That means the person who had something could not communicate while he was alive, so he tries to leave it on paper. The thing that I do not understand about this custom is that people act like such farewell letters are the most important things that they leave behind. What in the world did the person live for? I would like to ask what was he doing while he was alive.

If you live every day with *sutemi* in mind, you can show your way of life naturally. If you feel you have to leave a farewell behind it affirms that your way of living is poor. If the word "*sutemi*" has a negative image, I can change it to "desperate" or "devoted." I do not like to hear the expression "I want to live."

I teach the mind of *sutemi* when I give *godan* to my students. I let them sit, eyes closed with their back to me, then I swing a sword down on them. If they avoid this attack, I award them *godan*. If you become *sutemi*, you eliminate your vulnerable spots. If you become *sutemi,* your eyes, and ears, your whole body, turns into a defense mechanism.

IF YOU DRINK SAKE, DRINK BUDÔ SAKE

In the old days, people used *sake* drinking for rituals rather than for parties. By the era of Muromachi [1333 - 1573], *sake* drinking parties were for rewarding *bushi* who fought remarkably on the battlefield, which was called "*sake no kana*." On this formal occasion, the honorable *bushi* were presented with armor, trousers, and swords, and they exchanged drinks of *sake*.

One day I was asked to make a speech and *enbu* [*budô* performance] by the school of *Jieitai* [Japanese Self Defense Forces] in Asaka [Saitama Prefecture] in order to change the *kakuto jutsu* [military style of combat] of the army, navy, and air force. I accepted happily and went to Asaka with some of my students. Once there, I proceeded with my lecture, showed a *ninpô* movie, an *enbu* and answered many questions.

I emphasized the importance of *taihenjutsu* [body changing methods] because they use a short type of gun these days for *jukenjutsu* [bayonet skills]. As for *tankenjutsu* [short blade skills], I explained the readiness of *mutô* [no sword].

Kakuto jutsu, while we demonstrate forms of *sanpo hiden* [three ways, secret teachings: *happa, metsubushi,* & *suzu*], everybody started to get excited. At all events, the teachers of *kakuto jutsu* in the *Jieitai* are experts with confidence; therefore, *randori* is fun to do with them. After practice, I made a speech.

"It takes thirty years to master my tradition's *waza*. The soldier-trainees that you are going to teach are all amateurs of *kakuto jutsu* from my point of view. Therefore, you have to think upon how to teach them the defensive *kakuto jutsu* effectively, choosing sensible techniques that are easy and quick to master. I think that is your department in the area of *kakuto jutsu* responsibility."

Next came the *ninpô* movie. Laughter filled the room when the audience saw the scene with the *kunoichi* exposing her breast. After the movie, I made another speech.

"Gentlemen, you can't only laugh when you see the movie. In ancient times, it was said that drinking, gambling, and prostitution are three poisons. You must not indulge in these. No matter what strong *waza* you have mastered, if you have a weakness for these three poisons, you must still be called a novice."

In fact, the man who cannot handle drinking *sake*, women, and money is just like the weakest child, no matter how good at *kakuto jutsu* he is. The truly strong man can control these poisons easily.

After such an explanation I continued. "Regarding the ability to rule the country, they say Nobunaga for courage, Hideyoshi for wisdom, Ieyasu for *tanuki*. Courage and wit aside, it is difficult to be *tanuki* [crafty]. There's a phrase "*tanuki nemuri*" [feigning sleep]. This indicates the reverse side of the human beings who show their minds easily in front of the "sleeping" person. For instance, when a woman is sleeping, if the man sees her, he might show his lust. Just like this, if you pretend to be sleeping, you can see to the bottom of the enemy's heart and intentions. Then you can take advantage of his defenselessness. Therefore, you may call *tanuki nemuri* a kind of *shinobi juton* [animal-like escape]. You just cannot win if you do not have this skill of playing dumb." This ended my one-day lecture.

By the way, in the *budô* world we eat *oshiruko* [sweet bean soup] at Kagami-buraki [Japanese New Year ritual to cut up ornamental rice cakes]. Why do we do this? In my opinion, it is a custom of wisdom to avoid fighting in the *dojo*. If we only drank *sake*, it would cause fighting. I have never seen a drunk among the masters of *budô*. However, they seemed to enjoy *budô sake* [indulging in the martial arts].

LESSONS WE LEARN FROM THE DEMONSTRATIONS OF UKE AND TORI

The *budô* performance of *uke* [receiver] and *tori* [defender] is just like a couple [husband and wife]. If one of them does not do well, the other will not do well either.

I have many opportunities to be an intermediary for couples who will soon get married. I always say to the couple that the joy of married life comes from enduring while both are spiritually exposed.

Then I usually present them with one of my *budô* secret writings. For the one couple, I wrote:

> *"The water always runs down the indentation in the land, but that's just the beginning of the voyage."*

This teaches that when we get into trouble, there is no use crying about the situation. It is an admonition for the couple not to give up due to hardship, to try to find the mist (solution) in the air and continue to live vigorously. For another couple, I wrote:

> *"There is no village on which the moon does not shine, the moon lives in the mind of the gazer."*

Humans are egotistical beings. The newly married couple spends happy days, but as the years pass, they start to push their egos onto each other, and burn themselves up with insatiable desires. The person who cannot find happiness in his current life will never find it in his lifetime. You can have various feelings when looking at the moon, but the couple who gazes at it from their own house is the happiest.

At one of my student's weddings, I presented the message with this bookmark of happiness as a celebration proclamation:

"You and I are comrades who trained in *budô* together. You have truly become an honest and courageous young man through *budô*. Now we have reached the point for you to know that courage and honesty are not always the supreme thing. Too much courage pushes you to run amok blindly, and too much honesty makes you the fool of "stupid honesty" [Japanese expression]. Human wisdom combines the illusory and the real together, an important point to become happy."

By the way, if the wife is *uke* then the husband is *tori.* Once time when we performed a demonstration at the *Budôkan*, I told my students:

"*Uke* and *tori* are just like husband and wife. Unless the wife knows everything about the husband, he cannot perform well. It is very important that *uke* know *tori*'s *waza* and mind well — for instance, when the husband sits around and occasionally gives a gentle *kiai* to make the home peaceful and merry, and when the wife performs domestic chores well, she can build a great family."

Uke must know *tori*'s *enbu*, and at the same time he has to think how to make *tori* look great. This kind of consideration is important.

Moreover, when you have performed successfully *tori* thanks *uke* and shares the joy. When you fail, you cheer each other up. There is a saying that to marry only with *Bokuden ryu tenabe* [cooking pot with a handle]... I think that even a couple who are broke, quite penniless, can perform brilliantly on the stage of life.

I encouraged my wife to join *budô*. I do not think that to become strong and work out completely is the only *budô*. These are some of the important things to accomplish through *budô* training: learning your shortcomings, rectifying them, and spending your life full of joy. To practice performance for happiness is the true way of *budô*.

THE MOTIVATION OF PAIN

I do not know how many times I have been interviewed about my motivation for doing *budô*. I give the same answer every time. "I was born dead. Only when the midwife shook me head over heels did I start to breathe for the first time in my life, I heard. Probably because of that, I was a weak child. I visited doctors so many times it was like a family relationship. I had a nickname, *Soddapo* [dead branch], since I was skinny, pale, and nervous. In my early years, I was often fatigued and asked my grandmother to carry me piggyback. This lasted up to the first year of elementary school. It is a shameful and pitiable story. My basic motivation to become the man I am today can be considered as my reaction to my childhood inferiority complex."

However, the actual motivation was not like that. My life environment required me to have strong arms. My father was a merciful, righteous person, but once he got drunk, he turned into a knife-thrashing monster that could not even distinguish his wife and child. Besides, I was the only male in the house aside from my father. I had to become stronger than he was so I could manage to cope with his drunken madness and put him to bed. In that sense, my father made me learn natural *budô*, so I am grateful to my father now. My teacher, Takamatsu *sensei*, was also said to have been a weak child:

"I was called a crybaby and told that I was weaker than a girl. At school, I was forced to squat and pose like a horse while some kids sat upon me and hit my buttocks. They often made me cry. I had nine stepmothers since I was very little. My true mother and one stepmother were gentle but the other seven constantly scolded me and often were cruel. When I was nine my father said, "You cannot be a crybaby," and sent me to train with a relative, Toda Shinryukan *sensei.* I began as an apprentice. After a year, (I was in fourth grade) we were in gym class and my teacher called out my name to make me wrestle a classmate. I was reluctant to do so, but as I complied, my opponent fell over easily. I then threw my opponents one after another. My classmates and teacher were dumbfounded. After that experience I became confident, lost the crybaby label, and was elevated as a *taisho* [senior wrestler]."

Like this story, training can make human beings strong and sound. We often hear the story that somebody in *budô* training spends a certain amount of time in the mountains. The ninja trained in the mountains because they could hide from the feudal lord's killers and train in martial techniques secretly.

I heard Takamatsu *sensei* went to the mountains in spring when he was twenty-two years old. In China, *sensei* was called *Moko no Tora* [Mongolian tiger]. When he returned to Japan, because of beriberi and tapeworms, his family did not welcome him. He went into the mountains with a sick body, thinking he would die. He did not bring any clothes except those he wore and brought three sacks of brown rice for food. He settled at the bank of Kame [turtle] Waterfall in a hut without floorboards. He used fallen leaves and dried grass as a blanket. Since he did not bring matches he had to wash the brown rice in the waterfall, and he sun-dried the grains, crushed them, and ate them. He desperately chased nuts floating upon the water and ate them. His weakened legs were full of bloodstains.

One day, a *shugenja* [mountain ascetic] saw Takamatsu *sensei* under the waterfall and said: "You have tapeworms inside of you; I can free you of them." He chanted something like a spell and went away. After a week, tapeworms the size of *udon* noodles came out in three heaps. *Sensei* regained his health completely, ate nuts and fish, and concentrated upon the training of *Togakure ryu budô*. His partners were rocks, grass, trees, birds and beasts — in other words, all of nature.

After a year, his fingers became like beasts' claws; his superior skills became unshakable. It is however, not only in the field of *budô* that people sometimes get stimulated by pain; and it is this pain that often motivates people into the huge jump forward.

Especially when you are young, you should go through a lot of pain and make that experience a base. To find a vital purpose in life is important. Hideo Noguchi [1876-1928] became motivated by those suffering syphilis and became the world-famous bacteriologist and immunologist. Minamoto Yoshitsune lost his father a little while after he was born. He ran away when chased by Taira no Kiyomori and grew up training in *bujutsu heihô* secretly in the Kurama Mountain, and finally became a leader of the Genji [Minamoto] clan.

A person's real value can be judged during a moment of crisis. Life is full of symbolic walls and vacuums. When you encounter these points, you should encourage yourself, break through these walls, and continue onward. That is the way of the truly strong and brave man.

IT IS IMPORTANT TO BE IMMOVABLE

Even the notoriously violent Miyamoto Musashi had a few years of study and residence in a castle. The legendary Songoku [Monkey King] was detained in a rocky cave. There is a time in each of our lives when it is most appropriate to be immovable. This is like the earth experiencing only day and night. I think this kind of time is very precious in your lifetime.

I too had spent five years in vain when I got sick. However, looking back, those five years were an approaching run for a big jump; they were not static but fiercely dynamic. The people who become first class masters all seem to have a static era in their lives. Even under this static condition, only people who do not lose their fiery passion later become famous.

I am not trying to tell you how to become famous. I am saying that it is important to make an effort under any circumstance — stagnant, sickness, being in an unstable lifestyle, even when society is insane. You should consider such periods as an omen before you move again. Regard them as something necessary to complete before the beginning of a huge storm. I want to remind you that the longer the static period is, the greater the movement that awaits you.

When I was sick for five years, I could not even stand up. I sat at the *dojo* and gave lessons to my students. One time I was thrown and struck by one of my students, but I continued *keiko* with the notion of *"ninpô ikkan"* [enduring treasure, one joy]. Those five years raised my current *shinkiryoku* [spiritual power] and my ability to move freely.

When you are stuck on something, it is important to hold to your purpose but not press onward against the current. When you cannot move at all, try to concentrate, continuing forward as if in a boat switching to a stronger motor. The *keiko* that is most important when you cannot move is *kage no keiko* [shadow training].

BUNT FOR THE FASTBALL

> He notices *sakki* [intention to kill]. He evades in a flash. A few *shuriken* pass through the air right near his face. He finds a ninja throwing *shuriken* when he turns his face. A handsome samurai throws *shuriken* down onto the ground while he swings his sword left and right. Then he throws a *kozuka* [small knife]. The *kozuka* penetrates the ninja's throat...

This is a classic scene from a motion picture. The *kozuka*, which the Samurai used, is sometimes thrown as a substitute *shuriken*, but usually it was used to cut off a samurai's "top knot" or paper and used as a knife at meals. The basic *kamae* to avoid *shuriken* is called *totokuheushi*. Set the blade vertically in front of you and extend your arm forward, do not move the blade, and catch the *shuriken* as it bounces off. It is just like a bunt against a fastball in baseball.

Kusarigama is a weapon that attacks you from every angle. Even Miyamoto Musashi had a hard time when he fought against a master called Shishido Baiken. Baiken's *kusari fundo* [chain and metal weight] tangles up like a snake on Musashi's vertical sword *kamae*. Baiken pulls the chain little by little while he waits for the chance to cut Musashi with the big snakelike sickle. He steps forward trying to cut Musashi's neck. Musashi seizes the moment of Baiken's defenselessness, pulls out his *kozuka*, and throws it into Baiken's chest.

The other day, one of my friends who lives in America and who is the master of *kusarigama* visited me and said, "The *fundo* [metal weight] of the *kusarigama* is great. When I fought with a *kendô* master in a *kendô dojo*, he could not come near me with his sword."

When in a situation where you must fight someone with a *fundo* weapon, do not become too preoccupied with fighting and avoiding the *fundo*. The strategy to win this conflict is easy. All you have to do is watch the *fundo* carefully and then slowly deflect it with your sword tip. The *fundo* is like a rubber ball hanging by a string. If the person loses the timing of the swing, he will defeat himself instead. This is the essence of *kuden* on how to cope with a fastball. It is, in fact, effective to apply slow techniques against the fast speed techniques.

NERVOUSNESS PROTECTS AGAINST FAILURE

"You have to live in a courageous way. If you worry about petty things, you are being too meticulous, you will never become a grand person." Many people have similar expressions. Well, perhaps this one is true, but what does "live in a courageous way" mean?

In thinking about it, the expression is quite abstract, and if you follow the suggestion you may grow up to be a lazy, careless person. I am a bit concerned about this as people so often refer to *budô* for its good examples. However, this proves that some people do not understand *budô* very well.

When Musashi saw a horse, he never walked right behind it; he walked keeping a good distance from it. He knew the danger of being kicked with a horse's hind legs. Martial artists learn to naturally pay attention to what is around them. The public point of view upon this would be that the martial artist was "being nervous."

People in high positions with uncertain motivation always try to look good and display this facade, never showing their short temper or cowardice. Moreover, they try to teach such pretending as an important dictum to their junior workers. These men make miserable leaders. There are many things you have to be "careful" [heedful] of, paying great attention almost to the point of being nervous. Thus, it would be very kind advice to tell others how to be alert and careful.

However, you should not teach them to become nervous. This is a difficult point, but, in simpler terms, the nervousness of a martial artist is based upon his readiness to perform *seppuku* [ritual suicide] at any time. It is not the nervousness that comes from cowardice. Their nerves are impenetrable. Therefore, modern men must also have this kind of readiness and boldness in their guts, and at the same time, be careful — that is the important thing.

TENGU'S NOSE MUST BE BROKEN

You should not become a person that underestimates him or herself. We all like to walk on the road of life with great confidence. Be a little overconfident and become a bit proud. I do not think that is too harmful. I am saying you should always have a sensible amount of pride in yourself. I cannot emphasize enough not to become a *tengu* [Japanese arrogant demigod]. You must have enough self-esteem to encourage yourself from within, but you should not deal with others thinking you have more ability than you actually have.

How do *tengu*-people get this way? Because there are so many people who do not know anything, but think they do after reading or hearing some information and thinking they understand it fully. Neither people's hearts nor the real value of material things is measured so easily. Moreover, if you are to excel in one field, you must go through a variety of specialty training.

Bugeisha try to fast as part of their training. People ask them why they deprive themselves of eating. It is not about testing one's endurance for hunger. This training is to understand the preciousness of food. If you can easily get food, you never understand an appreciation for food. If so, you only develop the desire for more tasty food. However, the person who is in severe hunger will feel gratitude for food that the former group would spit out, saying it is no good.

By the way, what is the proper food for human beings? To learn the answer, martial artists fast to empathize with people who cannot get food. In this fashion, you come to understand that some people make a great sacrifice to get even the most modest of foods. It is not bad to purchase quality foods when you can afford it. However, only a person that really wants to understand the preciousness of food and eating can curb his desire even under circumstances when he is unable to eat. People that do not comprehend the preciousness of even the most modest foods will end up having difficult times looking for food that they feel is agreeable to eating.

Human beings must not become *tengu* [smug, conceited] in this life. If you should act this way, you should be lucky enough to have a person who breaks your long nose and helps you back into being a normal person. On occasion, I have told my students that they can act like *tengu* because they have made sufficient progress to brag about it. However, I tell them, if you want to become better, they should not wear the mask of a *tengu*.

GIVE HARD TRAINING TO REVEAL THE VULNERABLE POINT

When I was young, I was told that the first step of *shugyo* [austere training] is to endure the pain your teacher assigns you. Yet today, my point of view is that there is a bad tendency to be overprotective. So few modern men would flourish through true hardship. It seems like there are so many young men who want to stay in a nursery school environment and grow up without any discomfort. So they gave "*shigoki*" [arduous training] a bad name, and they consider their elders fools who give them a difficult time. It is an irritating phenomenon for me because I believe we cannot grow to be good humans without having passed through *shigoki*. This is not only about being good in the martial arts but also for developing into good people.

As seniors and leaders, we cannot force others to see our position by insisting that *shigoki* is right, but we dare not devalue our ethics through consideration of gentler living without any *shigoki*. I arrived at the conclusion that we cannot eliminate *shigoki*, so I decided to think of a new way for *shigoki*.

When I found my students' weaknesses, I criticized them sharply. Then they start to think that I am a traditional teacher and look at me with a sense of fear in their eyes. If I put off criticizing them, even for a few days, and then mention their faults later, some of the students feel they do not understand my intentions anymore. They wonder why I sometimes point out their actions immediately and feel it malicious to deliberately point them out. I think this is a trait of modern man; they hardly understand this *shigoki* as well intentioned.

When I called my students together and explained, "I never pick on your faults to annoy you. First, if I feel that it is useless to tell you your errors I will not say harsh things to you. In addition, you are only lacking in the ways I mention. If you rectify your weak points, you can be a wonderful *budôka*..." Their eyes looked at me with distinction. In other words, the phrase "you only have one weak point in you" really works. They work to rectify this point and commence to reveal their fighting spirit. If we cannot apply the old methods of *shigoki,* we must invent a modern approach to it. Students who cannot believe in their teachers are preoccupied with misunderstandings. Therefore, we have to enlighten their misunderstandings and help them find their good points.

DO NOT THINK YOU WERE UNDER SHIGOKI

During my early years of training, I never permitted myself to believe that I was under *shigoki.* I focused upon training and my lessons. This was because I wanted real self-development. The majority of people today tend to think they are under *shigoki* instead of being trained. They forget to better themselves or they depend upon others to compel them to get better. This kind of person never grows into being a big shark; they end up as a small shark that eats a big shark's leftovers. They cannot stand on their own and continue as regular students.

A big shark can only become the king of the ocean through self-discipline. When you become a big fish, small fish will not bother you and will hurry away from you. The life of a king can often be quite lonely. However, it is not the loneliness of being disliked. Being alone and being a part of a group is not a contradiction. The proper attitude is to train yourself, for yourself, and grow to be able to help others.

A trainer can use the word *shigoki*, but a trainee should not use it to describe his own situation. Instead of using an expression as *shigoki,* they should call it *keiko*. I sometimes do *shigoki* on *shihan* by irritating them verbally. I pick upon their weak points and *suki* [defenseless parts]. They become totally discouraged by this behavior. I leave them with their thoughts for four to five days, and then say something like:

"I am not solely focusing upon your shortcomings. If you think that way, you are not qualified to be a *shihan* [senior instructor]. The thing I want to say is that no matter how mature you are, human beings have imperfections and you should neither be angered nor disheartened when your weak points are identified. I am trying to help you develop *fudôshin* [immovable spirit], which means a mind not disturbed or upset by verbal mistreatment."

When you are under *shigoki*, if you feel unfortunate or have a spiteful mind like a demon, you are only a petty being and will never grow out of it. Only a person without an evil or vengeful mind can truly develop and endure *shigoki*. A person that changes his mood easily due to criticism during conversation will be kicked around forever in society.

In the movies or on television, they make a character that does not listen to his boss into a hero and depict other characters that always respond "yes" to the same boss as cowardly. However, if you think this tendency is correct, you are just showing your inferiority complex and weaknesses.

If you want to climb in your company's hierarchy, then even when you think your boss is wrong, you should follow his direction, and agree with his decisions. A man with a good profession and experience cannot be wrong most of the time. You should be like a golf ball. Do not resent your boss no matter how many times he sends you flying away. He will definitely come to you, like the golfer picking up his ball. Moreover, if you are very good, he will treasure you.

INTENTIONALLY BECOME A "BAD PERSON"

So many people believe a bad person will always harm other human beings, but I doubt it, because there is such a thing as a reasonable bad person [i.e. Robin Hood]. I call this person an *"akuto"* [idiom: aku = "evil" & to = "to grasp"; a person who understands this].

Once there was a saying that stabbing and robbing were just bad habits of the Samurai. However, this was how they survived in chaotic times and governed in such times. I met a politician the other day and he said: "It seems like I have a bad reputation and everybody thinks that I am an *akuto* [bad person]."

I answered "What is wrong with being an *akuto*? It is okay." I added, "There seem to be fewer people who understand the true meaning of *akuto* these days. I regret this deeply. Even Nichiren [Buddhist monk] had stones thrown at him."

"People do not pelt me with stones, but I constantly get called horrible names."

"Aside from that, it seems that a lot of modern politicians don't understand politics. I think the real politicians let those abuses be thrown at them and with determination of perseverance do the political matters."

Even those who are called *akuto* should keep their faith in the flourishing of humanity; this is very important for society. To achieve victory, a person may have to become *akuto* [grasp evil] but with these things in mind, he can still be a commendable "bad person." Leaderless *akuto* do not have a champion but all of the commendable *akuto* have someone they admire. Leaderless *akuto* will always band together to destroy a humane *akuto*.

An opportunistic person who tries to please everyone is good at pretense. Once he sees the disadvantages of a situation, he turns his back upon the community and goes elsewhere. This is comparable to a famous story about a man who was shamed in public because of his harsh words against unscrupulous social actions. Instead, he should be considered respectable because he retained his opinion while others pretended to agree with these corrupt social actions.

The more a person is a part of a scandal and makes enemies, the more he lives individualistically with a unique purpose. When necessary we become an *akuto* on our own initiative and live for other people. This noble spirit is lacking in modern *bujin* [warriors]. I call Kon Toko's [outspoken monk] harsh speeches "medicinal poetry."

THE BUSINESSMAN'S SOCIAL STRUCTURE

(The Epic of Toyotomi Hideyoshi)

I have a student who resembles Hiyoshimaru [16th century feudal lord]. He is different from Hiyoshimaru because his father is only an innkeeper. He always sorts his shoes neatly before he enters his home. There is a saying that the wading bird never muddies the water when it leaves. I think he has the potential to become an eagle. My wife also admires him, saying he is such an alert boy. Being alert is based strongly upon an individual's heritage and this type of person can be very good at *budô*, adeptly finding the opponent's *suki* [unguarded points] and scarcely showing his *suki* to others.

When the young page Hiyoshimaru (who worked at the castle gates) grew up to be Hideyoshi he formulated the strategy called *hyorozeme* [block the enemy's food supply], which does not injure either the enemy or his army.

There used to be a time when military forces mainly recruited energetic people. Today, in contrast, people with a higher intelligence have the best probability of being recruited. Why is it that people in athletic fields do not get priority? I think athletes are often great in sport competitions but they must have been poor aggressors upon the battlefield.

As training for new recruits, I heard that some military units were sent to the mountain for instruction in Zen or theology. In modern times, this would be meaningless and I believe it is more appropriate to train them in educated life because our society can be difficult to live in — for some it can be a cruel hell. If you want to reach an important position in this hell, you had better become like Momotaro [mythical character who befriends animals that later help him fight demons].

Momotaro had a monkey, a pheasant, and a dog. The monkey excelled at wisdom, vicious wisdom. The pheasant had an ability to predict earthquakes. By predicting an earthquake, which is more frightening than thunder, fire, or a boss, you can calm the bosses' contentious mood. The dog looks faithful but it can become like a ninja and smell the differences at work, using various means and tricks.

The first requirement to live well and reach a higher position in society is to practice these three elements of each animal as your body and soul.

When it comes to money problems and contracts, company men often lose their credibility by being concerned with petty matters and failing to understand their customers' real needs. They need *waza*, a small one for important individuals, a big one for very important individuals. It is likewise with fishing. If it is a small fish, you catch it quickly, but you have to have better timing for bigger fish and wait a considerably longer amount of time to catch them. This is a form of *nin* [perseverance], so to speak.

As the proverb goes, "Let them cut your skin, and cut their flesh; let them cut your flesh, and cut their bones; let them cut your bones, and cut off their life." Should they take your life, let your integrity remain.

This applies to modern society, as well — if you want to reach a higher position, you have to work three times harder than others in your position do.

Do not complain for the sake of complaining. Devote yourself to your endeavors. The paths in front of you will begin to open. Do not be defeated in our society where flattering people get top positions without much effort. From when you begin working at a company, if you have a beggar's attitude, you will not attain a high position.

If you become tired of being a company man, then it is time to leave that job. You may need some radical changes in your life.

MAKE OTONASHI NO KAMAE

I am not saying you should be utterly indifferent and be silent while you let others do all the talking. Rather, it is better for you to openly say what you really feel and want to say. When it comes down to the nitty-gritty of a situation and you have judged the circumstances with a cool mind, take *otonashi no kamae* [posture of silence]. Remember the old saying, "The weaker the dog, the louder its bark."

Some people say such a dog is useful because it barks a lot but it will soon end up only as a noisy dog. Moreover, when you watch the dog barking you can see his cowardice. The dog puts its tail between its legs and looks like it is going to run away. I do not want you to become this kind of human. On the contrary, the heart of a person who bangs his fists upon a desk or kicks a chair is weak and filled with distress. Just like a strong dog will suddenly bite into an enemy without making a sound, from a silent *kamae* I want you to have real strength.

It is a mad dog that bites all the time, but human beings have a reasoning intellect, which a dog does not have — the point I want to emphasize is the mental state of readiness in a crisis.

I equate the mind of the martial arts with the expression "the hand is faster than the mouth," but I do not want this to be misunderstood. Do not waste time arguing for petty things, and be ready to use violence in a fight to the finish, if it is over something that is truly important.

To put it simply, do not make a big deal over casual or tiny problems. If you continue to do this, nobody will seriously consider your smart speeches about important issues.

Human beings are said to be emotional creatures. This is certainly true. The emotionality of human beings can be heard in the things I say. There are many cases where little situations grow into big problems when you are emotionally sympathetic. I do not think there is a need to waste time on such petty things. When you realize you put too much emotion into something or talk about it too much, instantly assume *otonashi no kamae*. The opponent will be scared by it and you can sort out your own mind too.

ATTACK WITH SHIN-GI-TAI IN HARMONY

To unify the mind, technique, and body [*shin-gi-tai*] is considered the most important thing in the world of *budô*. If you can accomplish this, you can enter the world of selflessness. In this exists the *bujin* [divine warrior].

The other day, I saw Roger Williams' piano performance on television. The performance was wonderful and although I am ignorant about piano technique, the feeling of the performer playing the piano with his whole body moved me. If the technique of piano playing comes from his fingers, his fingers and his body looked like they were one, it appeared that Roger Williams was dancing with the piano.

A kindhearted man of *budô* must not place limitations upon his martial ability, in this way he can live in harmony of mind, technique, and body. This is essential.

I have heard that there are many men who try to do these things, this unifying mind, technique, and body, just like apprentice monks... living like fleeting clouds and flowing waters. Some people do things well although they are trying to do more than one at a time. This age prizes such cleverness. However, we must acknowledge that if any part of our mind, technique, or body is absent then we cannot pursue our goal to true depth. Any job that is performed by doing several things simultaneously has little *kokoro* [heart] in it. Lessons that lack *kokoro* do not have much to offer or inspire people regardless of how excellent a technique is involved.

On the other hand, to unify the mind, technique, and body is not so easy to do. Even if you are conscious of it, that does not make them unified. In addition, even professionals find it hard to keep a continuously harmonious state of being. The mind tends to become disturbed in daily life. Even after we learn how to prevent our minds from becoming agitated, we never entirely erase our troubled feelings.

I do not urge you to strive for this to be continuous in your daily life. Rather, I encourage you all to have this focus when you are prepared to do something. Singing a song is quite the same. A good singer should always try to inspire his audience but this does not always happen. If they do not put spirit into their song, the song seems lifeless. Nagishima-*san* as Mr. Baseball is worth watching even if he is in a severe playing slump. Why is this? It is because of the attitude with which he devotes himself to one thing, playing baseball. That inspires people.

BE A TASTEFUL ACTOR

Life is a drama without a performance. A drama is only complete if it has a beginning, middle, and an ending. This means that we are the main characters in the drama of our daily lives. In the drama of life, as in a theater, we should study the principal character rather than the acting. You must view your personal drama on the stage of life. However, if it does not have a plot, you cannot study the acting or think how to make your role more appropriate. In truth, you must be able to show your real character all the time. I may have been a bit wordy, but to put it more simply, do not be vain or two-faced.

If there is a person who crudely betrays other people, those individuals close to him will become disloyal to each other and this makes a depressing environment. This kind of person coolly deceives others — expresses his drama, eagerly acting them out. "If things turn this way, others will go that way, and then how will I get anything out of my life?"

In a sense, these people can be called materialistic. If you trust these people, you will never make a difference in your community. Therefore, sometimes you may have to deceive these people. As previously explained there are times you must be a bad person [*akuto*] rather than good. However, if you act this way for too long a time, people may feel justified in naming you a truly bad person. Please try to understand this notion.

These days, there is so much dishonesty among people that it has become an inclination for many people. Some people believe that being able to lie well is a factor in deciding a person's importance.

Currently, people say "to brown-nose" is the way to obtain a better place in their work hierarchy but this kind of person can only be the servant of a bad administrator. A great boss will be watching you even when you are not flattering him. You should not be a monkey in a monkey show. The elegant character's acting will not ever be forgotten.

GIVE ADVICE INSTEAD OF GETTING ANGRY FROM THE HEART

My teacher taught me, "Do not get angry from your heart at your students." I did not understand what it meant at the time. I thought it would be natural to get mad if the student did wrong and, that he would not be a good person if I overlooked it. However, I have recently begun to understand this statement. The emphasis is on "from your heart" rather than on "do not get angry."

For example, if one student caused an accident or problem, there must be a reason or a motive, and it often turns out to be quite different from what seems to be upon the surface. For instance, I had a student whom I believed was bad but he was not, and on another occasion, I thought a student was training with the wrong partner. In addition, some students with natural ability or talent sometimes conceal others students' mistakes. If you criticize them without inquiring after their explanations, you would not be a proper teacher.

If you are in a position to be a mentor, is it not a good idea to keep this method of reprimand deep in your heart? Not only does this help our next generation develop but also helps establish a sound relationship with your colleagues. To be firm, you need not get mad from the heart. If you really get angry, you become blinded by your emotions, which should be avoided because it hinders your ability to understand other people's motivations.

The people who work for a respectable boss often have the feeling that they "depend" upon him. They expect that their boss would overlook and repair any of their excusable blunders. With this kind of feeling in their minds, if they were scolded in a harsh manner, they would have conflicting emotions over you and their associates.

Once emotions collide, truth, justice, good, and bad all vanish. An ugly dispute will follow in which all sides defend their positions. It is most important that you try to avoid these situations for growth and encouragement of the inexperienced employees. The main reason is that it is very difficult to regain trust or repair the damage that this type of situation brings to a work place. It is best to approach the difficult party with the attitude that he can correct what he has done. In this way, he can regain some pride in his work. One motto in my *dojo* says not to be angry from your heart and not to injure your training partners.

TEACH PEOPLE EVIL IN ORDER TO KEEP THEM FROM EVIL

The big job for management is to obtain good employees. Parents who raise children, teachers who educate students, seniors who encourage newer employees — I believe there may be many different ideas and beliefs, but the most significant wish of all is to encourage people "not to become corrupt."

Many people say that you have to keep employees away from corruption, and educate them not to do immoral acts in order to teach them correctly. I am very opposed to this idea, although there are many people that think this way. I do not contend that it is an inherently poor method, it is only that my primary thought is that if an employee does not understand what evil is, you cannot force them away from doing it.

It is important to have a positive attitude and strive for proper action. However, once you step out into society, you may not necessarily see what is "proper." Your environment is filled with people who care little about you. There are not many people like your parents or teachers. Under such circumstances, how can a person who does not know the ugliness of evil overcome it? An utterly admirable person is prone to fall victim to evil, because it appeals to him as an attractive thing, since he has not known it before. There are many examples of this in the everyday world as well as in the world of martial arts. I recall the story of a martial artist who had flawless sword techniques but could not use of them because he did not have a good understanding of their harmful effects.

I believe we need to understand the difference between knowing evil and being drawn into evil — they are totally different things. Most often people are drawn to evil because they are unaware of it — that is the way of our misguided youth.

I sometimes intentionally show my students books with erroneous information. They struggle for a time but soon learn to judge if a book is good or bad and avoid paying further attention to the bad ones. It may be an exaggeration to say they do not pay any attention to the bad books but in time, they learn to be less indecisive about which is good or bad. Some people have an aversion to mixing good and bad books [or people] while others prefer to rid themselves of the bad ones. But this proves those people [teachers] are lacking in courage [to take on the task of teaching and helping both good and *akuto* people].

In order not to be immersed in evil, you have to comprehend evil and then you can develop a strong spirit to dispel its darkness. If you do not go through this process during your period of spiritual training, I believe it would be too late after you have grown and matured. One thing to keep in mind is that a teacher has to judge for each individual student, whether it is better to teach him or her "evil" or good first.

THINK BY YOURSELF

To provide protection for his staff might be the role of the senior executive in a company. It is a role for parents to offer their children advice when they are discontent. However, if the advice is too simplistic, you are best off not giving them any suggestions.

In ancient times, a person who strove to learn *budô* would do individual *keiko.* After learning skills from his teacher, he trained himself to master those lessons. He had to have a determination to study through the techniques while alone. Going into the mountains, he would repeat his solo training in nature, fighting with animals and trees.

These days, so many people forget to "go into the mountains." These people tend to desire the easy way out. If they are having problems that are complicated, they immediately ask someone older to solve it for them. Moreover, the elder gives them easy advice. Most people answer nicely because they think it would be good to help the situation along, but in fact, this often ends up hurting the individual's growth.

It might be a little different from *keiko* in *budô*, but some problems can only be understood by the person who has the problem. An advisor gives suggestions trying to solve the problem through applying his own experiences, while the listener (who does not have those same experiences) listens to the guidance as if it were being received from some divine being. There is sometimes a serious danger in missing a lesson's important point. Therefore, you should sometimes offer the advice, "Ponder the dilemma yourself." You may consider this "coldhearted." However, being cold illustrates the need to solve a problem [finding warmth]. Perhaps, some days later, the individual will return saying; "I can't figure out a solution..." and he will recount his problem in a totally different manner than his first telling. You will now be able to discern how to offer advice that is more appropriate by judging from his revised account.

In *budô*, we inform students of the proper answer after the "torment" of making them think for themselves. Some things must be learned through suffering or they will be forgotten for the rest of your life. We all must learn to solve our own difficult problems. Furthermore, in *budô*, we suffer great pains to master the best techniques. It was through the pains and labors of our ancestors, who became the founders of our traditions, that these unique techniques were invented.

RUNNING IS FOR WINNING

Mr. X, who is a *yodan* in judo, visited me and asked this question: "When you have to fight against a hard striker, how can you win the match?" Indifferently, I countered his questioned with, "What will you do when you are attacked by a rhinoceros?"

"I think I would run away; it's scary."

"Then, that is the answer." I said.

Mr. X was dumbfounded for a while; "But there is a time you cannot run, right?" [Hatsumi:] "I do not believe that. If so, you are lacking the knowledge of how to run away from a rhino according to its behavior."

The basic spirit of a martial artist begins with the lesson, "When you see the enemy, win by running away." Hot-blooded young men are willing to fight, but the people who teach the young must have the spirit of "win by running away" under any kind of circumstances.

When you have to fight as a man, except on special occasions, you can run away. A person who rarely gets upset can control the lower part of his body well. He learns to dodge any attack by shifting his lower body. There is a way to dodge an attack by keeping the upper body (especially the mind) calm, using good timing, maintaining watch of the opponent, and avoiding the attack through use of the lower half of the body. You would be a matured individual if you achieve this proficiency.

"But I get so angry," many young people say. Then you should answer, "To lose your temper is be a creature lower than human."

When someone gets very upset, the lower body turns rigid like a stick. Moreover, they start to attack their opponent with furious attitude.

"Have you seen animals when they get upset? Both rhinos and bulls lower their heads and dash into their adversary. If you do the same, forgetting how to get away, that proves your mind is no better than those animals." If you heard this, you must understand the true meaning of the phrase "win by running away."

BE AN EXPERT AT SOMETHING RATHER THAN A JACK OF ALL TRADES

The world cherishes talented individuals. However, like the phrase, "Jack of all trades, master of none," you must know that to be handy invites poverty. To be versatile is only useful in convenient situations; instead, you often realize that you have notable skills.

In general, a versatile person is bright. Moreover, bright people think out their actions before they actually act, and then execute them without any additional motions. Therefore, for an employer, this is the most beneficial person to have around. They must be praised: "You can do the job swiftly. Your mind is really sharp." Moreover, for a while you may get a lot of work and start to think that, someday you will become a big name, since so many people recognize your ability.

However, things do not always go that way. There are many cases where this kind of person ends up used as a convenient troubleshooter of which others take advantage. However, it is impossible to advise these versatile and bright people to be inept. What can they do? They must have spirit and believe that if they excel in one thing, they can master a hundred things.

It is not easy to excel in one thing. When you concentrate upon one thing with all your energy, you will become stuck with unimaginable difficulties, for which you thought you had prepared. It might even be unnecessary for the problem that you are trying to solve. Therefore, versatile people must take into account that they should ignore all other thoughts and solve the central problem first. Perhaps, they cannot pursue the problem too deeply with that attitude. To become an expert on one thing, they must focus and overcome their problems through all out effort. This then leads to developing one's inner mental abilities. Once you access these inner mental abilities, you find (in spite of yourself) that you can work in numerous areas by adapting to your environment. In other words, you become an expert in hundreds of fields.

BECOME A POPULAR PERSON

Whether it is good or bad, I want you to examine the desire to become popular. I do not like this type of aspiration. But if you are offered a popular position [at work, in school], and it is beneficial to you, it is best to ride the tide and not mull it over.

In modern society, there are many short cuts to become a successful and popular person. In the world of mass communications such as television, a wise person learns "to rides the trends." If you cannot adjust to modern trends, even with excellent ability, you will not be able to function well in society.

Sometimes, it is difficult to view famous people with an impartial eye, because in order to get publicity, these people sometimes have to conceal and expose themselves. They appear as mannequins without any soul. Often, these people become famous overnight. As long as this exists, we must admit that there is a kind of mastery to living a high profile social life. To illustrate, some people study very hard to become a Parliament member but fail because they are not famous. On the other hand, once you become famous on television, you can easily become a Parliament member. You might as well master the system necessary for your individual advancement.

For the most part, I have been advising the reader to follow the opposite path. However, in life, there are many times when it is justifiable to be inconsistent. You should come to make use of this idea for other events and for matters of the heart.

Some readers may become offended because I mentioned the rare case of changing careers from television personality to Parliament member, but the important thing is to become a person whom other people appreciate. Obviously, it is inappropriate to show your true emotions all the time. If there is a way to gain a bit of credibility because others value you, it is through emphasizing your good traits and trying not to show too much of your unfavorable background. In order to do so, you must constantly pay attention to your behavior and keep them acceptable.

BE BOLD, ACT TIMID

A doctor who has known me for many years said, "Often you act very bold but at other times you look timid." I was very happy to hear these words and could not help smiling to myself. The reason is that having both of those qualities is necessary for genuine warriors in the martial arts world. This seems to be evidence of my developing into a real *bujin*.

There are big techniques and small techniques in the world of *budô*. And it is not always the case that big techniques beat everything; it is a fact that sometimes small techniques can beat big ones.

Overall, the nuance of the word "timid" does not give us a very distinguished image. Some people who do not know the real meaning of the word say, "I don't want to be a timid person." Too many people say such things. If you look the word up in the dictionary, "*shoshin*" [timid] means to pay attention to many small matters; this is not the usual meaning at all.

We should all become people who pay attention to small details while being bold. Some may think it is not manly to be timid and cautious, but this is not so. Being bold and being timid are fundamentally different. Even trying to mix the two elements, while you are trying to be bold on the surface, the quality of being boldness will crush the timid side. To pay attention to detail or be gentle and warm can only be done by a small, timid person.

Contrived meticulousness is an imitation that does not move anybody. Every human has bold and timid qualities from birth. However, those who cannot understand the decency of being timid try hard to eliminate that aspect of their character and become unbalanced, brazen people. This is an unnecessary undertaking. The ideal is to have a male natured boldness with a female gentleness and warmth, for dealing with people.

I believe this is the best way to balance our lives. In *budô* there are the sayings, *kajo chikusei* [flower heart, bamboo spirit] and *banpen fugyo* [myriad changes no surprise]. If we take the former as timid, we can translate the latter as bold.

DO NOT RUSH TO BUILD A HOUSE

So many young men want to build their own houses. I understand the feeling. I watch the problems they face after learning it will cost more than half of their salary for rent. But, this matter aside, I want you to hear my thought, "Do not rush to build a house."

I am not saying it is bad to own a house. I would like to say to wait until the house will easily build itself. Some may say, "After waiting too long, we will not be able to build a house. We must invest our money in spite of financial difficulties..." It does sound reasonable.

However, I fear that there is a strong materialistic desire that drives their lives crazy. I think it is better not to have a house rather than go through all this pain. If you start to think of life based all upon loss and gain of money, you will lose your humanity.

As your child grows up, he wants to have his own study room, so you managed to build one. Nevertheless, is it a study room in the truest sense? In terrible cold wind, Ninomiya Sontoku [19th century "peasant sage of Japan"] studied with books in his coat while carrying firewood upon his back. If you do not have the strong desire to learn, your environment will not matter. For Sontoku, the firewood upon his back might have given him patience; the blowing cold wind might have been his own remorseless path.

When your desire to build a house grows, I want you to remember this story. I think you need to focus on your direction, understanding the situation that you want to have a house, but you cannot afford it.

Some people may ask, "Why can't we simply endure the pains despite owning a house?" But the former is spiritual perseverance while the latter is patience for materialistic goods. There is a notable difference between these. The former patience could be a springboard to the future. Nevertheless, the latter only creates pain, which will leave nothing afterwards.

Of course, in the end Ninomiya Sontoku came to own a home called "Ninomiya Castle." I do not think we can all do the same. In our lives, we all must bear certain burdens and physical trials. In my experience, I had a very hard physical training with Takamatsu *sensei* in the Butokuden *dojo* in Kashiwara. This helped me become the person I am today.

SOW GOOD SEEDS IN A GOOD RICH FIELD

Good seeds sometimes will not grow in a bad rice field and even if the field was good if the seeds are bad, they will not grow either. The seeds that I am referring to stand for you and the field could be translated as your work place.

In other words, no matter how great a talent you have, if you were among bad people or an aggressive company, society cannot help but regard you as one of them. When you can insist, "I'm not like them" and act accordingly, you are treated differently. However, you should never forget that your environment affects you and in spite of yourself, you may lose all the good things that you have. Talent (seeds) will grow taking nutrients from the environment. If the nutrients are bad, the seeds will not grow as they should.

Therefore, if you have a good seed, you should sow it in the best rice field that you are able to find. Several times, I have met people who had their names printed on the business cards of a major corporation and were quite proud of it. These people are sometimes lacking in etiquette, acting as if they are fearless, as long as they carry the name of that company. My impression on such occasions has been "Why is this person so rude? Even though he is the member of a major company, he seems to be very ill-mannered." In other words, under the circumstance previously mentioned, people can overlook aggressiveness if you act appropriately, but in this case, we tend to look at people that act bad in a good environment as acting very discourteous. This is a generalization our society makes and it is a probably a poor way of judging people.

Perhaps in the former case we need to give these people more credit. The public can judge the exception right away but in is difficult to notice the exception in a large environment. The differences are difficult to see; they are hard to catch. It is not good only to grow big like a tree, but we would like to grow soundly in our lives. In order to do so, you have to make sure your seed is good and find a good field in which to sow it. If you can do this, you might live a wonderful life just like a perfect wind pushes the yacht forward.

BECOME A PERSON WHO CAN USE MA

Mr. Musei Tokugawa (1894-1971), who was called the "God of Storytelling," used to say the life of storytelling lies in *ma* [interval]. Even if you told the same story again, a person who knows *ma* well will make the story come alive. However, if you put bad *ma* in, you will kill the story and it will become *ma* [evil].

Living in the world of *budô*, which places great importance upon *ma*, we must understand this notion. In *budô*, this *ma* can be used as a tremendous weapon.

Ma is the moment that you see when the enemy starts to attack. At the same time, it is a moment for you to have confidence before you start to attack. In addition, it is an important component of jointing actions of the past and the future. Therefore, *ma* is not only a pause but also the life of action itself. You must cherish this *ma* in your life, too. There must be *ma* between one action and another. I do not want you to regard it only as a "pause."

Some people say when they finish very demanding work, "I'm going to empty my brain for a while and I do not want to think about anything at all." But if your mind were too empty, you would be too slow in starting your next task or assignment. At the same time, if you try to go directly to the next action, it will unavoidably cause excessive pressure on you. So you should take an appropriate *ma* and try to control the one in the past and in the future.

For instance, what reaction do you have when you see an erotic scene in a movie — you are far from adept if you get very stimulated when you see common sex scenes. This is because you did not have the proper *ma* between seeing the erotic scene and your reaction. In this case, a person should apply proper *ma* in order to consider the incredulous things going on naturally in our nation as a flow of the world. He should take *ma* between his instincts and his thoughts to consider why there is a society that allows one thing to happen and another not. This then would offer a great value to the fact that someone saw an erotic movie and became uneasy.

DISGUISE YOURSELF USING BÔJUTSU

You should know the essence of *bôjutsu* as a method to proper living. Depending on its use, a mere stick can do a variety of tasks.

For example, if you approach an enemy's territory with a *bô* in hand and with silent footwork, your enemy would instantly deem you are coming to attack. However, with the same *bô* used as a walking cane while you are limping, the enemy would misconstrue your intentions. Whether or not you plan an attack disguising yourself as a disabled person, you can use this strategy in other situations. One *bô* can be used in many ways if you simply apply your fantasy. This method of *bôjutsu* strategy is called *ihen no bô*.

If you see the opponent is afraid of your *bô*, then it would be a good strategy to swing the *bô* hard, while if he looks at it with disinterest, it would be useless and tiring to swing the *bô*.

So, strike at the enemy's vulnerable points using this nature of *bôjutsu*. It would be too naive to consider the *bô* as limited to the actions of swinging and thrusting; hit strategically.

We live in a very complicated modern world, but I treasure a person who is upright like a *bô* and I would like to insist that you should live like the *bô*. However, if your nature is to count upon others to be as honest as you are, you must learn to be more careful and doubt them.

In other words, when you use the *bô*, I would like you to choose the *bô*'s position as if, when the opponent has a *bô*, you think he is going to use it on you.

If the opponent is taken aback by your *bô*, you immediately think he has lost his spirit to fight against you. However, if you yield a big "*suki*" [vulnerability] the opponent's *bô* might be immediately drawn out toward you. Also, if you should be struck, there is no use crying about that to the opponent or calling your opponent cowardly names. Impressions of the fight aside, if you took a hit you lost the fight. The opponent outsmarted you.

Even a young man such as a "*deku no bô*" [useless stick], when he endures in society long enough, can become a strong *konbo*-like [hardwood staff] man someday. By doing so, an ordinary man can become an extraordinary man.

CHAPTER FOUR

MEN AND WOMEN

THE ATTRIBUTES OF WOMEN AND METHODS OF SELF DEFENSE

In our modern society, it is common for both men and women to be deceived by the opposite sex. When this happens, it not only destroys the individual, but also their family as well. In ninpô, a person who acts in this fashion, falling whim to the seductions of another, will lose the power of this training.

Kunoichi techniques were taught not only to women; there were also cases when men used these techniques while disguised as women. A long time ago, a Japanese warrior, disguised as a woman, neared his opponent who was a practitioner of *Tai Chi Chuan*. The *Tai Chi Chuan* person assaulted the disguised man and was immediately killed by *her* sword.

The basis of *kunoichi ninpô* is the attractiveness of the female form to males. What is the nature of this attraction? A person by the name of Ayame Yoshizawa, wrote a *Kabuki* play called ***Ayamegusa*** and stated that these are the items that female impersonators [*onnagata*] should consider: "Proper demeanor is the most important lesson; the only lesson that should truly matter. The reason for this is that men are born with a natural ability in deceptiveness. These men must appear as *keisei* [courtesan; prostitute] and act a bit inattentive toward men. So, they must practice acting in this fashion."

To be a *keisei* means to be beautiful and to be a seductress, not a woman that is very serious. The important element is that there is an attraction for men when a woman is a bit inattentive to them. Each of these *keisei* were intelligent and received a comprehensive education. If this type of woman neared a group of men and acted inattentive, all of the men, even those normally uninterested, would be charmed.

Learning basic gestures is the foundation of emulating a woman's charm. Gina Lolobrigida, the famous actress, said, "It is more important for women to act radiant yet reserved, rather than to act too intellectual. The size of your bosom does not matter. Whether you are sexy or not depends more on your personality than your appearance."

Marilyn Monroe, a famous international actress, knew all of these things. Therefore, she posed with her lips seductively, sent innocent side-glances, and enchanted men. This fascination was the foremost power of the *kunoichi*.

A short time ago, my students and I filmed a movie and included *kunoichi jutsu*. In the film, a man tried to attack a *kunoichi* who was walking alone in the mountains. She ran toward some nearby bushes to escape. Realizing that there was no evading her attacker, she lured him closer by revealing her bosom. The *kunoichi* found an opportunity to knee her attacker in the groin. As he cringed in pain, she grabbed the man's hand with a *kakushi* [ring with thorns], threw him with a *gyakute* [wrist reversal], and ran away. The man chased her again, caught her, and tackled her to the ground; he spread her legs as he pinned her down. The *kunoichi* relaxed her body pretending she had given up. The man reached out with his hands, and at that moment, the *kunoichi* struck him with *happa ken no ichigeki* [open hand strikes to both ears] and escaped having left the injured man on the ground in great pain. This is one of the most important self-defense techniques for women.

Kunoichi jutsu is used mostly by women against men. This required the *kunoichi* to learn about the structure of the male body. A *kunoichi* needed to know about men's weak points and how attack those weak points when necessary. In this, there are two main types of attacks: physical and psychological. Physical attacks range from *kogoroshi*, *oyagoroshi, metsubushi*, and *happa ken,* to the form called *fudo kanashibari* [*see* **About Kiai**].

Psychological attacks are those that are affected using the six senses. For example, visual attacks which are done by woman not wearing any undergarments beneath their dresses. *Kunoichi* find it easy to attack men by way of their senses.

Most men like [admire] the female form. *Suki* [likes] can also signify *suki* [unguarded points]. When you like someone too much it can become a weakness and drive you crazy.

When men are the targets of a *kunoichi* attack using *miryokujutsu* [attraction techniques], most men lose their heads. This too is a secret of *kunoichi ninpô.*

When I was acting for a television show, my wife demonstrated some *kunoichi jutsu* techniques. One such technique, *namazu zuri,* uses a weapon with a fishing hook that is attached to a man's groin. Then the connected cord was attached to the person's leg, so that should he move he would hurt himself badly. On another day, we introduced an old weapon that cuts off a man's private parts.

Mr. Nakamara was asked if he drinks. He answered, "No, I can't do that." People who do not drink can act drunk better than those who do drink. That is because they can observe drunken people well.

The reason why *onnagata* (men who perform as women) can sometimes express even more feminine allure than women, is probably because they can observe women better.

The *Sennin of Kume* turned into a normal person after he gave himself over to a female. The ninja can detect the techniques of *kunoichi* because they never give themselves over to a female. Whatever you do, do not lose yourself.

One should not be off one's guard although the opponent is seems weak. This strategy fits best when it encounters *kunoichi ninpô.*

By the way, since I have written about *kunoichi ninpô*, let us speak a little about sex. One cute young lady said, "*Sensei*, my chest is so flat, is there anybody who will love me?" I said, "Young men or men who do not really know about females say that a flat chest is not attractive. Do not worry. Maturity is more important for women. If you had a plate full of food and it all tasted bad, you would not eat it. Yet, if good food were served in small amounts, you would keep asking for more."

"It is not that bigger is better, or the more you have experienced is better. If you think something was tasty, that is all that truly matters. A beautiful lady like you needs to be more confident of yourself. Then I am certain that you will look more beautiful and be more desirable."

Another girl then said, "My boyfriend has a quickness problem when we make love." I said, "These problems are common when men are young. Do not worry about it. Do not tell him and have him worry about it either. I think both of you girls have been reading too many bad magazines."

Then another girl said, "I heard there are many men who are on strike [impotent]." I explained jokingly, "That is sad. I feel sorry for men that have had trouble with their labor unions." Then I said, "There are a lot of men that have similar problems and that may be why the divorce rate has risen. I met a man who went to a doctor for help and had no luck, so he went to a soapland [massage parlor]. He said that the women there were much more professional than most therapists were. They truly knew how to help him. It seems that there are quite a few men that have found cures at those places."

Anyhow, I see a lot of articles written about sex, but what surprises me is that people really do not know much about sex. Many people do not know that mastering one technique fully is much more important than mastering forty-eight different techniques. Many men in our society feel that when women become forceful, they lose their sensitivity. Up until recently, men perceived frail women as the most content.

LOOK FOR A SPOUSE WHO UNDERSTANDS SEPPUKU

You might think that this is a terrible thing to say. You might think it is very stupid to commit *seppuku*, and that you would never want to keep that sort of person near you. Some people might laugh that suicide was a bad custom during the feudal period of Japan. But are there people that can commit *seppuku* in these modern times? A long time ago, *seppuku* was one of the ways to protect one's family, country, and honor. In other words, it was the best way to show your love and virtue to your spouse. The head of the household is always carrying the burden for their families. So, *seppuku* was the way that their spouse could show respect and honor their attitudes toward life.

How about people in modern times? Maybe they can commit *seppuku* with their marriage partners, but I do not think they can commit *seppuku* alone, all by themselves. Some married people seem to want to live independently and be wealthy by themselves, even though this harms their families. This may only be a small part of a person's desire but if someone were to marry this kind of person by accident, they would suffer all their life. *Jigai* [variant form of *seppuku*] was intended to harm only the individual. Rather, *jigai* should bring something good to society, or to people. The *jigai* of which I speak is not something of hysteria or something that has to do with mental derangement. A person who can commit *seppuku,* which is to say a person who has this kind of bravery and commitment, will be a good spouse. Even if we do not understand the behavior of cutting one's belly with the *tanto*, people today should at least have this mentality. People say that a woman changes depending on their husband, but a man changes, too, depending on his wife. I want readers to marry a spouse with bravery such as to commit this type of *seppuku.*

THE MISTAKES OF LOVE SHOULD BE DISMISSED

Musashi rejected the love of Otsu to live his life by the sword. Ittosai was cheated by his wife, and never accepted a female's advances after that. He then lived by the sword, too. The sword, if a man has it, gives him the image of living life strongly, but if a woman holds it, gives the image of malice.

By the way, if you analyze love physiologically, it is just like foreplay before you conceive babies. After a child is born, the mother's love will be divided between the love for the husband and the child. I was asked about my view of love as a martial artist. I answered that truth is more important than love. Then the questioners said there was truth in love, also. I replied that I did not believe in the doctrine of love for love's sake, but do believe in the idea of martial arts for its sake. That means I see love from the martial artist's point of view. There are numerous types of love. Some people do not have true love because their minds are mixed up. For example, a husband works very hard but he buys his wife expensive clothes. Then, his wife is not dressed up for him but for other men. These spectacles occur often in our society. In foreign countries, people say love can make a "dead" person come alive. It is possible for this kind of love to kill just as easily as to restore a man to life.

If a couple commits dual *seppuku* and one of them did not die, would the survivor be happy? The happiness of love will be fruitful if the couple is consistent with their life together. Love between a man and a woman is just like the relationship between a bow and an arrow. They do not work without each other. It is important to shoot for the target of happiness together. Happiness is the situation when men's and women's hearts and bodies are satisfied. Likewise, when the love is full and ideal, it will keep a couple happy forever.

DECEIVE AND BE DECEIVED

Love is getting back together and breaking up, deceiving, and being deceived. I want you to mature by being deceived by the woman you love most or by a man, you trust most. People often grow better by conquering those trials. When I was young, I fell in love and had my heart broken. Now I laugh at myself, saying that I was foolish. But during that time, I really suffered. Now I am writing this manuscript while laughing, and reflecting, looking in the mirror at myself as if I am very young. Now I think of my vexation for being deceived by a friend, whom I had trusted, as very childish, and I do not feel any hatred toward him.

It is strange to say, but when I saw him after a long time, it reminded me of the sweet memories. In a long life you will cheat and be cheated by people. People who hold onto hatred after being cheated, or hold onto joy after cheating someone, will not be able to improve themselves, because they shoulder these burdens [hatred or joy]. It is important to grow as an adult who does not deceive or become deceived after cheating someone or being cheated by someone. You feel awful when you have to deceive, and your burden is greater. Therefore, remember that it is important not to deceive people.

But it is not always a heavy burden if you lie to somebody. If you can make people happy by deceiving them, then it might be fine. A husband and wife are always deceiving each other. By doing this they make a home together. This is a normal marriage. By the way, the ninja were said to be strong in lovemaking. This is because they knew themselves and their partners, and they were always trying to discover each other. That is why I think the ninja and his wife blended very well. Furthermore, the ninja protected his weak points and made up for them with merit. After the ninja mastered one way to attack, he learned to use these methods without disclosing his ability to his enemy.

FRIENDSHIP BETWEEN MEN AND WOMEN

Friendship between a man and a woman is wonderful. But it is difficult to keep friendship between an adult man and an adult woman. A long time ago, people said, "Men and women should not sit together after they reach the age of seven." You should believe that men and women truly need to behave this way. Nevertheless, young people today are very relaxed and casual about this. That is good. Friendship between men and women... there is always sex tension between them, but they do not seem to deal with that. There are, of course, perils everywhere. Therefore, it is important to respect each other's rules and to know each other's character. It is important to enrich each other as all good friendly relationships do. If friendship between men and women turns into Plutonic love, it is a heavy sickness, just like a crazy person who does not think or realize that they are in love. Meanwhile, getting rid of the feeling of love is thought to be manly, like a Samurai. Because falling in love is the same as the faith that makes you accomplish any one thing. And cutting this faith off shows you have a stronger faith, which is to go in an important direction as a man.

PLAYING AND HEALTH

I do not like people who are not playful. What we do in playing is useful for keeping good health and getting rid of stress. But there are a lot of traps or blind spots in playing and many people do not notice them. For example, some people start playing golf after becoming middle aged. They think it is good for their health because they walk a lot and the air is fresh. But golf has a lot of quick twisting body motions so starting in your middle years has a high risk of breaking a bone or getting muscle strain. This is also true of bowling. Twisting bodies or getting tired because of using too many muscles or nerves causes a lot of trouble to the internal organs. Sitting too long hurts your back. Staying up late is the worst thing you can do for your health. Some people might rebel, saying we cannot do anything if we think that way. However, what I want to say is to think about what you do according to your age. Moreover, you must have a certain rhythm in what you do.

If you play at what is no longer good for you, it is no longer a pleasure. I thought the nature of playing [for recreation] would change due to inflation, but one day I realized something important while watching a kitten. Although the kitten did not have enough room to play, it always found something to play with. When it got tired of playing too much, it would rest. Just like that kitten, we should play innocently and then go to sleep. This is the best way to play and is useful to better your health. The pleasure of playing for money [gambling] will accumulate stresses and is unhealthy. You would be best to stop this kind of recreation. The same thing can be said for the playing around between men and women [unsafe sex]. You should stay "clean" [disease free]. If you boil water with coal, you can quickly boil bath water. However, this will harm the [old Japanese style] bathtub. If you use wood, the bathtub will last much longer. The same thing can be said about hormones and food. If you get too much you will become overheated, and it will make you get old faster. Playing too much can make you grow old fast and shorten your life. While playing is good for health, you should do away with the playing that will harm your heath. Be careful not to die while making love!

FROM SEVEN VARIATIONS TO SEVEN DIFFERENT COLORS

My wife started wearing black clothes after a clothes designer told her that she looked very nice wearing black. When I noticed this, I unconsciously thought, "It does not look good on her at all." A few days later, the designer visited and told me that my wife looked good in black clothing. "Isn't this so?" Mentally I thought, "Why should she be wearing black? She is not a ninja or anything..." Then my wife said to the designer, "My husband thinks that it doesn't look good on me at all." So I said, "If you wear black in a messy house like ours, you will look like a witch [demon] in the western world. But it would be nice if you wore that at shrines and such."

That is, clothes will look fine depending upon what "setting" you are in. If you do not have this sense of "seven changes," custom will perish.

Anyway, many women think of their clothes first, even before their own life. After they get dressed, they wonder what other people think of their appearance. That is why there are many worried women. In a bad relationship, men cheat, and in a good relationship, they like change. And they behave according to these changes. Women find it easy to figure out male behavior; they are creatures of habit. Imagine there is a woman who does not like the idea of sex. However, she wears exquisite undergarments because of her sense of beauty. Yet, it is obvious that she does not understand a man's desire at all. Even in my day, we had Sunday through Saturday [clothes] so that people learned to adjust to changes and thus, prosper in love. This is *henshin no jutsu* [metamorphosis methods] in *ninpô*. Do not forget that there are cases when you have to change according to the circumstances, and there are cases when you have to change against them.

LOVE WITHOUT RESTRICTION

I have heard that some young women today have casual sex with just about anyone, and check their partner's sexual abilities before they fall in love. This is because they do not want to find out that their husband is clumsy in sex after they are married.

Religion, philosophy, laws, etc. regulate the rules between men and women. The rules in the sacred books are different in each country. Many people think that *iai* [quick draw] was done with a *katana* [long sword], but sometimes the short sword is more useful than its longer companion is. When a Mito clan Samurai at Sakurada Gate killed Ii Naosuke, it was said that Ii could not draw his sword because of the handle's cover. I do not believe this. A master of the art [of *iai*] could have taken care of himself in spite of the cover. The same could be said about a man's private part. You do not have to be concerned about size. All depends upon how much you have practiced and your skill. The same can be said about a woman's abilities. Whether you are good or bad depends on feel and technique. Everybody has different strong and weak points. It is important to know these and make use of them.

By the way, striking a weak point very hard can sometimes cause death but, on the other hand, if you hit the same point softly it can sometimes cause pleasure. I do not know if this is a good or bad thing but it is out of date to think that making love can only be performed in a bedroom. Everywhere are the places for having sex, such as cars, under a blue sky, and on an airplane.

There are many different sexual preferences: sadists, homosexuals, and lesbians, etc. The forms of love are endless, too. There are no rules in love. So, there cannot be any rank in love. That is why you must be very careful.

You cannot say that the person who has practiced long can improve and master it. This can also be said in the martial arts. Reasonable practice makes you improve. That is why good-looking women and men do not always make good lovers. There is a story of a tragedy about a girl who was very ugly but fixed her face up and became very beautiful. This did not make her happy because her lover left her after finding the deception. Yet, she still loved. The meaning of "there is no accounting for taste" is that people's tastes differ individually. If we try to force rules onto love, those rules will be thrown to the dogs.

A LIE IS NOT A SIN IN LOVE SCENES

This happened when I walked around in Yoshiwara with my senior student. "If a call girl comes up to me and pulls my sleeve, I will go with her on this street, but I am sure this will not happen." My student was listening as I spoke. Then, several of the call girls did come to us but none pulled upon my sleeve. They turned around and went away. "See. I told you." Nevertheless, as a man, I did feel rejected. They must have felt scared thinking that I was the head gangster or the mob. I was walking like one, too.

"This is also martial art training. But this is not enough, next time when I come I will walk so that they will pull my sleeves."

Often, my wife forces me to promise that I will buy her something, like "this or that." Or that I will do "this or that" for her. But when I do not feel like going to get her anything or doing anything, I just leave it undone. Then my wife complains that I am a liar and cannot be trusted.

"Men are liars. If they go out, they have seven meetings [many distractions]." "If they do not lie, they cannot live," I said. I think we have to lie sometimes. Women are often made happy by those lies.

It is good to pretend you have forgotten your promise, if you were to meet a girlfriend you did not want to see. Don Juan is an expert at deceiving women. I have a student who worked in a bar. According to his experience, if you say, "you are beautiful," to an ugly lady, a smile and money will come to you.

Even if you did not enjoy having intimate relations with a woman, you should say it was good. A large quantity of those lies would enhance your lovemaking later. Small lies are one of the wisdoms of life.

GOOD USE OF RISQUÉ HUMOR

Most people enjoy risqué humor and the people that able to tell these jokes. This is a simple fact and it is not bad that people feel this way. Sadly, in Japan, it is not favorable to speak or quote men and women directly.

There should be joy in the martial training, that is why we have playfulness in ninjutsu. A dirty joke is universal humor. It is not too much to say that character can be judged by the way you use a dirty joke.

Even at a dinner party or at a business talk, a little bit of racy humor can bring merriness and will be able to catch others emotion. When you are sharing these tales with women, you should tell them in rhyme.

One time when I spoke with the grandmaster of *Goju ryu* karate, Ichikawa *sensei*, we spoke about the *sanchin no kata*. He was saying that the more we do *sanchin no kata*, the less we live. At that point, I observed, "If you use *chin* [male organ] in one trench, you can live much longer." We both laughed.

DECEIVING WOMEN, KUNOICHI NINPÔ

The life of a woman, as well as a man's life, is directed by natural tendencies. One can be successful or not, depending upon the use of their natural talents. One thing I have noticed is that when many women gather they are fastidious [in their judgement of each other]. They think that misconduct with the opposite sex is the worst of crimes. However most of these women love to watch soap operas during the day, and deep down, they aspire to be like their television heroes. In simpler terms, they are as "dirty" as men are. Because of these things, some modern women are unbalanced. One of the measures of a woman's interest is her passion. But some modern women lack this passion as if they have become allergic to men. These women do not know how disappointed men are when they wish to share passionate embraces with a woman but are rebuked with only dismissive looks.

That is, too many women think only of themselves, and are very selfish. In the old days, both women and men knew how to please each other. They were artists in the field of lovemaking. That was why they valued each other so highly. Modern women should take advantage of their feminine characteristics and be considerate to men, as modern men remember the proper way to treat women. In this way, I want all women, young ladies, wives, and older women, to be "priceless women." Priceless here implies "a complete woman." If you can honestly say, "I am a priceless woman," you would have passed as an elegant woman of ancient times. Some women cry a lot. That weeping confuses men. This was a secret technique of the *kunoichi.* Women who knew how to weep when necessary were useful to coerce men in bargaining matters. The desirability of these women depended upon how well they could cry and how authentic it sounded. A *kunoichi* was a superb artist at the use of crying and causing men to become entrapped in her web of deceit.

LEARNING METHODS TO ATTRACT A PARTNER

You have to use a counterattack in order to lure a woman. However, if a woman becomes attracted to you and you are unable to politely discourage her advances, you will never be liked by any woman.

If you were to write a common love letter, it would be in vain. An unusual letter would work, though. If you write something like, "I'm burning with passion for you. I want to share your nights," and if she did have a crush on you, she would be yours in a moment. In the martial arts, you will encounter people to whom certain weak point attacks will not work. This will confuse the beginner, but the experienced person will be able to instantly find and attack another weak point.

You had better not believe a woman's weak point is one that you read about in magazines. You have to find her weak points by yourself. It is not something that you ask someone. Finding a woman's weak point is a great discovery for a man and it is the best way to develop a relationship. A man who does not do this is not qualified to truly love a woman.

A METHOD TO BALANCE LOVE

When we talk about the intensity of love, it does not mean that you must love only one man or woman forever.

Recently, a law which protects animals has been passed and it makes dog and cat lovers very happy. I wonder if anyone recognizes the fact that dogs and cats are eating other animal meats. People think of love selfishly. I want people to have love beyond that point. Love that offers no self-sacrifice is not true love. I have heard the line; "I love you. That is why I want to know more about you." However, what if doing that hurts people? In this case, you would be better off saying, "I do not want to know you better." There are many types of love between men and women.

NO REASONING IN RELATIONSHIPS

The less intellect there is between a man and a woman, the better the fight they get into. Yet, they will also make up sooner. They fight forgetting themselves, that is why there is nothing left after they fight. After all, the fight between a man and a woman is like the fight between positive (+) and negative (-) polarities. Intellectual or rational fighting always leaves hatred or jealousy after they are done. I want men and women to exist as intellectuals during calm times. But when it comes to fighting, you should both empty your head. Argue until your heart is content.

The challenge of attracting a partner has an element of a nervous encounter, both physically and mentally, but you should try to pursue any possibility worth your integrity. The courtesans of ancient times devoted themselves to earning a man's attention through learning poetry, music, dance, tea ceremony, and even religion. Even modern *geisha* study golf, horse racing, politics, etc. Men are generally vulnerable in the area of lovemaking, while women are often vulnerable in the area of relationships and material matters. You have to grasp these essential differences and an appropriate way for getting your needs met while fulfilling your partners' needs.

You can often find surveys about male-female relationships in current magazines. There are so many different kinds of surveys and statistics that I think all this "studying" has gone too far. People seem to be unable to help themselves. I believe that I have mentioned this a few times, but do not be confused by those magazines. No matter what they report, no matter what surveys they do, it will never change the fact that men crave lovemaking while women crave relationships and material goods.

Denshô

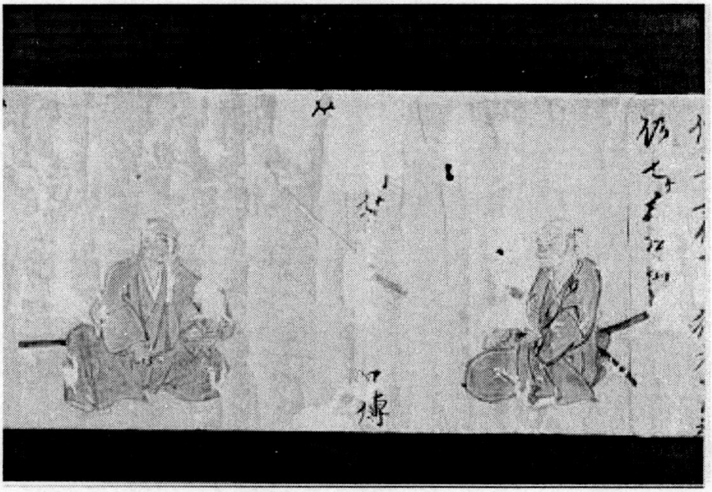

CHAPTER FIVE

NINJA DISCUSSION

THE CONCEPT OF ZEN KEN ICHIJO

Many people associate modern *budô* with Zen. However, this limited viewpoint exists because Zen thinking was held to permeate Samurai society. This viewpoint was foremost in the minds of many swordsmen and thus has survived over the years. In addition, earlier Samurai were strongly influenced by the teaching of Shotoku Taishi [crown prince and perhaps the most influential ruler of ancient Japan] and Honen [famous Buddhist monk].

For example, the phrase from Shotoku Taishi's Seventeen-Article constitution, "Cherish the harmony among people" is assimilated into the *Gyokko ryu* idea that "*Bushin* [the warrior heart] cherishes the harmony among people."

Similarly, the teaching of "Respecting *Sanpo*: *butsu, ho & so* [three treasures: Buddha, law, monk]" is interpreted into *Togakure ryu*'s *sanpo hiden* [*moriban, shinotake, & tekagi*]. Zen teaching says to endure embarrassment and disperse regrets. This is called *ninniku seishin*. Also, Honen's sect wrote, 'cut off the bad karma of regrets by using your body.'

As you know, Honen was born a child of a Samurai ancestry. In Hoen 7 [1142 AD.], when he was nine years old, his father was killed in a night attack by Akashi Sadaaki. In that era, it was virtuous for a child to avenge his parents' death, but Honen became a monk in an effort to find a way to save both himself and the enemy, too. It would not be wrong to say that the concept of *zenken ichijo* [Zen and the sword are one] were born in the latter part of Samurai society.

PURPOSE OF SHUGYO PURPOSE OF LIFE

A martial artist trains toward the ultimate realization of *budô* and makes an effort to grow from this. Recently, I have come to believe that death is the same as sleep. Therefore, there is no desire or regret. On the occasion of Takamatsu *sensei* death, there was no desire or regret.

A physical body dies, disintegrates, and transforms into something else, as will the Earth someday. Therefore, it is a laughing matter to think too seriously about the life and death of humans.

The *gokui* [essential teachings] are elusive; the *gokui* look easy to grasp but can actually be very difficult to understand. The feeling is just like that of being a jellyfish floating in the ocean. The same can be said about the *satori* [enlightenment] of the martial ways. It would be most appropriate to float about in the common world.

Takamatsu *sensei* used to call himself senile and then drift about in the air of Kashiwara City, drawing and painting, and finding joy in it. This is to drift and feel the existence of the world, empathize with flowers and enjoy the harmony, and to reach heaven as a live human being.

Therein, lies the key to solving the purpose of *shugyo*.

One day I was training with a foreign student who was returning to his home country in about six months. Another student said to me, "He cannot master such a difficult *waza*. He will only suffer pain." Then I said, "That is correct, he will not easily master this *waza*, but I am trying to give him spiritual strength and confidence within this short period. Then, after he returns to his own country, he can refine his techniques with this confidence that I have given him."

In the *denshô,* there are descriptions of *shoden* [beginning level], *chuden* [intermediate level], *okuden* [advanced level], and *gokui*, in that order. My students practice these *waza* one by one. After about ten years, they will master most of the *waza*. I tell them, "The *waza* described in the *denshô* are only elementary ones. Do not fool yourselves, no matter how good you are, into thinking that you have completed the *menkyo kaiden* [license for completed mastery]. You would be better off thinking that the material you completed was simply *shoden*. Then when you finally graduate the training, it is like mastering *chuden*. *Okuden* is the real life from then on."

This notion is not limited to *budô* — in modern society; there is the idea that it is all right to master things by degrees [levels]. This notion prevents the infinite goal, and divides life, study, and art and thwarts a person's growth. [Mastering things by degrees] makes it hard for people to focus upon an infinite purpose. This is a terrible reality.

ON DIVINATION AND FORTUNE TELLING

In ancient times, people made predictions about natural disasters and prepared for warfare. Initially, they studied the changes of animals and plants and found ways to make predictions. For example, if sparrows enter the thicket or stay high up in their trees after busily eating food, or if insects start to enter buildings, or carp jump up out of the water, or frogs start to croak, it is a premonition that rain is going to fall. On such an occasion, we prepare *uton no Jutsu* [methods to exploit the rainy weather] or battle in the rain. This could be making soldiers' movements inaudible to the enemy by the sound of the rain or generally taking advantage of the sound of the rain.

If a bird hastily flies back to its nest and stays there, it is an omen of a high wind. When insects that live high up in trees come down, or when skylarks fly low in the sky, or when the leaves of reeds stick out sideways, these are also omens of a high wind approaching. Just like these examples, nature gives humans warnings in various ways.

Thus, one strategy called *"tenmon"* [heavenly gate] was formed. In Chinese *kenpô* [fist method], there are styles called *Pa Qua* or *Tai Chi Chuan*. These words indicate a meaning of *hakke* [divination] or the essence of creation.

Chimon [earth gate] is based upon whether the day is a nice or poor day. These wars involving strategies using *tenmon* or *chimon* and using the judgment of fortunetellers occurred in ancient times.

Yet now, even with radar, this "fortuneteller war" continues. Today's trend of divination is also a sign of it. It seems like there are so many people who are driven crazy by onomancy, physiognomy, palmistry, fortune telling from the aspect of a house, and fortune telling from the family crest.

One day, an onomancy teacher named Nishikioji Masanari [Kyoto, Japan] told me that my name shows very bad fortune; it is the same bad name of the person who was killed like Rikidozan [famous pro wrestler who was stabbed to death]. I am a human too; it bothered me and I started to study onomancy myself. Gathering up seven *ryuha,* I realized that my name has good points and bad points. Then I picked peoples' names from newspapers and magazines who died in strange ways. I found out that even people with a good name — number of lines, arrangements, and *in-yo* [*yin-yang*] spirit — died in accidents.

However, I could not chase away these worries because I was suffering autonomic ataxia [imbalance] and psychosomatic problems. During that time, Takamatsu *sensei* sent me a letter saying "It is bad to have the '*yoshi*' in Hatsumi *Yoshi*aki. The *kanji* '*yoshi*' can also be read '*masa*,' so you had better change your name to *Masa*aki and print that on your calling card."

I noticed that people like Kiso Yoshinaka, Minamoto Yoshitsune, and Oishi Yoshi all accomplished major work, but they experienced misfortune afterwards. I used the name Masaaki thereafter. Since onomancy has a strong influence (self-hypnosis) upon one's own feeling, it might be good to change your image sometimes.

Bujin also did "*nawa bari*" [cordoning off with rope] during castle building, which is like what a construction planner does. Therefore, they studied the system of "divination by direction," too. The direction called "*kimon*" was most feared. Therefore, on New Year's Day, the *daimyo* asked to receive a name plaque from the Kuki family to avoid place at his *kimon* [demon's gate]. Emperor Godaigo named them Kuki [nine demons] because they were stronger than nine demons. I think that is why they used their plaque to dispel the "demon's gate."

I, myself, am not a blood relation to the *sôke of Kukishinden happo hiken*, so sometimes I inscribe a plaque to avoid evil and bad directions. The families that use this name plaque seem to live peacefully. *Kigaku* [the study of air/ambiance] alters the mood by changing the air in the room. Also, if your home does not get much sunshine, you can set up artificial sunlight.

In *heihô* [combat strategy], fortunetellers are sometimes employed. In addition, soldiers sometimes use fortunetellers to make it look like they are winning the war. For example, if you take for granted that the enemy will not come to attack because today their fortune is bad and thus you do not pay much attention, the enemy often will come to attack due to this absent-mindedness and win the war.

In *gunryaku heihô* [combat strategy related to positioning] you must ignore fortune telling in order to win. In daily life too, you must train yourself to be strong and make an effort to have faith yourself and not be swayed by divination. It is better to change your life with your own potent mind rather than with fortune telling.

Fortune telling works, after all, only a small percentage of the time. Even a patient abandoned by his doctor will survive if he has more than luck in life. The most famous fortuneteller was stabbed to death. Why don't handicappers place bets on their own horse races?

The effective prediction of war by fortune telling requires knowing the percentage of correctness for fortune telling. To win beyond mere fortune telling, you must have a strong spiritual power to beat it [therefore beating the odds].

Divination should only be used as a reference. Even the master of divination considers thirty-percent correctness to be a great percentage.

Everybody is annoyed when they see that their fate is the worst. However, this "worst" can turn into good luck. Mr. Nezu Kiichiro has the worst luck, according to onomancy. In spite of that, he is living a most fortunate life. As you see in Dante's **The Divine**

Comedy, to go to heaven from the last circle in hell shows that the worst luck can turn into best luck.

There is a saying that people go to Daishi-*sama* [famous shrine] to lose bad luck but instead they return home carrying bad luck upon their back. A proverb says that good and bad luck are entwined like a braided rope. Find a way to live joyously, unconfused by divination.

FROM INDIA TO CHINA TO JAPAN

A young man from India came to visit me to study Japanese *bujutsu*. His eyes looked like a hawk's, his limbs were like a mosquito's limbs, and he looked like a fighter. He was a surgeon who came to Japan hoping to learn karate.

I am a *rokudan* in karate. When I taught him some *kata*, he was so happy. A few days later he asked me to teach him my *bujutsu, koppojutsu* and *taijutsu*. I did some training with him. His techniques were precise as needed in the basics of *kobudô* [old martial arts]. For instance, when his kick came thrusting toward me, he would crouch low like a cobra. I dodged with *taihenjutsu* and applied a bone jarring strike. I was sure it would make his body ache over the next couple of days. As I expected, he called me the next morning to say, "My body is shattered. I am in too much pain to even get up." The techniques he used are *kusute* (most practical *waza* combining judo and Aikido), *wajikoramusute* (iron hand), Kalari *taijutsu*. However, I do not think there are too many people in the world that can do these techniques correctly like he did.

In addition, my Indian student could use a staff called "Solonbo," *barumokoru* [short staff], *muchan, kusari fundo*, sword, hatchet, and *shuriken*. He could do our *ninja aruki* [ninja walk]. This is a method of walking when you have to go a long distance or when you are tired; he called it *porinara*. He told me his *dojo* was built on the ground with large holes and with a roof over them, under which they would do physical training.

"Do you know India's old sheep keeper? He carries a staff and walks or runs over rocky mountains. He can walk about ten miles without any difficulty. Most of these people are masters of *bôjutsu*. They are very fine *bugeisha*. There are many foreigners going to India to study *bujutsu*. Nevertheless, those people are only introduced to the professional wrestlers in the cities. The professional wrestlers in India are not martial warriors. They are only showmen. The real martial warriors live in certain areas away from the city. The professional wrestlers never leave the city. This is because if they go to the countryside they will get killed by the real warriors."

My Indian student, who spoke in a very unexcited way, mastered all his country's martial talents, which we call *bugei juhappan* [18 martial skills] in Japan. People say the Buddha and his disciples were all masters of *kenpô* [fist method] and *bujutsu*. Probably this extended to "*dô*" [way] in certain ages.

It is said that in China there was a *bujutsu* 4,500 years ago. The origin of *zutsuki* [head thrust] was the headpiece of Shu, a chief of a savage tribe. His copper headpiece had an iron forehead and horns, and he stabbed and destroyed the enemy's body with them. Also in Chinese *kenpô* there is said to be a connection to *hanetsuki* [battledore and shuttlecock] and *kemari* [football], which explains their dexterity.

They say Emperor Huang Di trained soldiers with the game of *kemari*. In later years, Chinese *bujutsu* would be divided into southern sects, Canton Prefecture and Fukken Prefecture, and northern sects' *bujutsu* centering near Kahoku Prefecture and Santon Prefecture. Today, they are famous as Shorinji *Kung Fu* and *Tai Chi Chuan*.

In Japan, it is said that Chingen Fu, who was naturalized as Owari Tokugawa, taught *kenpô bujutsu*. However, according to several *denshô* and *kiki*, there was a Japanese *bujutsu* even before that time. Thereafter, hundreds and thousands of *bugei* traditions were born and as time went by, they developed strong cultural and physical characteristics.

It is a sad part of human nature that although you have a great art of your own, other arts always seem to be more appealing, and you desire to go to other countries and learn their martial skills by *shugyo*. When I finally said to my Indian friend, "Your country's *bujutsu* is really wonderful. It is great. Please reconsider the essence of Indian *bujutsu*, and do not get too involved with Japanese karate, for the pride of India."

He fully understood this and, in time, returned to his country. From India to Japan, and then back again to India...

BUSHIDO AND ART THEORY

The phrase "I found that the philosophy of *Bushido* [code of the samurai] is to die" is very famous. In reality, a Samurai never rushed to his death. Furthermore, he was to overcome the notion of death and live as long as he could. And when the time came to die, he would not leave any regrets and die happily.

Once *seppuku* and *hara kiri* made sensational news, but why did people commit *seppuku*? A simplified explanation would be that *seppuku* was a method of dialogue without words. Samurai act like Samurai and never speak, and then they cut their belly to communicate and to cry out. It is body language. Moreover, it is a decision to protect the social order by nullifying one's existence without words. Some people think *seppuku* is unique to Japan, but this is not so.

Plato said that soldiers should die, hence killing their ideology. This also helps to build a peaceful society. *Bushido* is an expression of the sacrificial spirit in order to protect the most important ideals. In other words, we cannot protect our society without *Bushido* spirit.

Should we not regard the *Bushido* spirit as important in a society filled with egotism, like ours? Regarding *Bushido* and art, the art that emerges from a warrior is beautiful; in much the same respect as Japanese *Bushido* is beautiful. The sword, the *bô*, the spear, and calligraphic works were born and have survived in various traditions. This is magnificent.

How about today's art, in which the spirit of *Bushido* is absent? Did this art bring progress or change? Modern artists believe it has.

However, today's world is in trouble. The artwork became very abstract, literally reflecting our harsh modern realities. When I see abstract paintings, I feel like I am witnessing the destruction of the Earth. I want many people to have the *Bushido* spirit, *yamato damashii* [the Japanese spirit]; the more the better.

LET'S GO GENTLY

Zen — the encyclopedia explains it as "one of the important goals in Zen Buddhism, is to reach an ideal state of mind in *gedatsu* [salvation]..." However, it means no such thing.

The method of *fuza* [sitting cross-legged] is to straighten the spine and breathe through the belly. It is also effective generally for maintaining good health. You start to understand *ninpô ikkan* when you achieve mental patience by sitting for a long time. The value of looking about one meter ahead with half-closed eyes is to teach you that if you open your eyes fully and try to look far, you may not recognize the *satori* right around you; it is a kind of affirmation. As Zen monks say "katsu!" [cry of enlightenment], *Budô* also has *katsu* [reviving methods]. A *katsu* [cutlet] is related to shish kabob but it is a kind of *ichi gyogaku* [devotion to severe training] to enliven people.

Taira Saemoni Yoritsuna ordered his soldier to cut Nichiren Shonin's [1222-1282] neck at Tatsunokuchi [Ishikawa, Japan]. Yet, the stalwart executioner was blinded by a strange light (some say he was hit by thunder) at the moment he tried to cut, and he could not do it.

I believe that the executioner might have been scared by the legend that if you kill a monk your family will be thereafter cursed for seven generations. Also, I believe that such an elevated monk as Nichiren must have had formidable spiritual power or the willpower not to be afraid of death.

In my *dojo*, the students practicing for *godan* should be able to avoid the sword from behind; *rokudan* or *shichidan* should read the enemy's mind; *hachidan* and *kudan* should move or stop the enemy at will. Probably the high priest Nichiren Shonin had mastered this *hachidan* and *kudan* ultimate technique. I give the answer "to die" when I am asked what *Bushido* means.

It is a cliché, but let me speak about this since there is currently a prophecy craze. When you attain the ability to make your mind empty or to feel like you are dead, you cannot be tempted by divination. Because you do not exist — therefore no one can foresee your fate by divination. That is a truly strong man and one who can create his own fortune for himself.

There are many *injutsu* [invisibility methods] in *ninpô*. To state it plainly, this is to be enduring with unwavering persistence. An evil person is prosperous for a while; this is fact. Nevertheless, he will definitely perish, and this is a reality as well. To put up with evil while it is thriving and to learn to recognize its realities is *injutsu*.

Some people have regrets their whole life, blaming a man or a woman who betrayed them. These people's minds are similar to a mind that aspires for revenge, but if people were practicing *injutsu*, they never think of revenge as an immediate solution. They can live each day with peaceful minds.

THE CAMERA LAUGHS

The existence of the slow-motion camera allows accurate judgment of sumo, horse racing, etc. Therefore, I thought that it would be a good innovation for the development of *budô* to use the camera, and I made some mischief.

There is a technique called *kawara-wari* [breaking tiles] that is breaking twenty tiles at once. One of the karate *sensei* said that the fist can punch through tiles, so I experimented. According to this person's story, when you break the top tiles, the bottom tile has to be broken instead of the middle ones. However, when you see it in slow motion, twenty tiles broke from the top to the bottom, in order.

Next is an experiment with the bow and arrow. One of the teachers of *kyudô* [archery] said that when you release the bow after pulling to make a full-moon shape, the arrow flies but the string does not follow the arrow. Is that true? The answer was "no" based upon the results of his experiment. The string and arrow are pulled into a full-moon shape, and the string follows the arrow until the string makes the shape of a crescent moon, then the arrow is released for the first time.

I must say that a slow-motion camera offers an excellent eye to study *bujutsu*. This eye is especially important for the people who study sword unsheathing, kicking, throws, and such fast-moving *waza*.

However, no matter how fast the strike or *iainuki* [sword drawing]; it is only a superficial technique. This technique can be studied carefully by the naked eye. Therefore, the *waza* that will be invisible to the enemy's eyes is really the fastest *waza*. It is not a matter of the speed of the *waza*. Even a slow *waza* is effective if the opponent does not recognize it or it can be a fast *waza* that the naked eye does not perceive. In other words, it is important to train knowing there is an inner technique [*ura waza*] that can deaden another persons' mind and eyes.

Yagyu ryu's seigan no kamae is set by standing straight and making a wide stance with the shoulders and feet and then aiming the tip of the sword toward the opponent's eyes. Takagi Oriemon, who was defeated by Yagyu Tajima no Kami in a match, climbed up Eizan [Hiei mountain] determined to challenge Yagyu's secret sword methods, and asked Sounryu [monk] for a method to achieve victory. "Forget everything else and keep training. Just train yourself..."

After Sounryu told him that, Oriemon sat by himself in the evening mist of Eizan. The days passed as he trained and meditated. One day, he was drawn into sleep. The moon was shining brilliantly on the valley. In a dream, the marvelous scenery enchanted Oriemon while he was standing in a clearing with a spear held as a walking stick. Then a sudden gust of wind pushed black clouds to cover up the moon. Oriemon just stood in the dark and could not move his body. Suddenly he heard the growling of many beasts. The growling startled Oriemon; he awoke from the dream and opened his eyes. In spite of himself, he ran to Sounryu without wiping away the night dew that drenched his body, and told him the dream. "Is that right? Well, now that you have perceived such things, I have nothing more to instruct you."

Oriemon went down the mountain with his head hanging down. Sometime later, he had a rematch with Yagyu Tajima no Kami, but neither could strike the other and the match was a draw. This episode proves that both men had such a swift mental grasp of each other's intentions that they could not actually make the moves because they were always past them in their minds.

Aside from a slow-motion camera, another important tool needed is one for long distance sight. In other words, it would be possible to see different perspectives from a close shot using the *gokui* of *senrigan* [clairvoyance]. It is the *satori* of *shingan* [mind's eye].

MOROKU KENPÔ AND GOKETSU KENPÔ

Moroku kenpô [olden fist methods] implies not showing others that you have trained in *budô*. I often see people striding down the street like tough guys, but a master of *budô* can easily judge that sort of person's actual ability and their weaknesses. [*Goketsu* = courageous]

This is a Chinese tale... One day, when a young farmer was working in the field, a monk came up to him. "I am a wandering monk and am having difficulty because of sickness. May I ask to stay overnight at your house?"

"You must be in deep trouble. You look weak." The farmer invited him into the house. The monk fell asleep in peace and stayed in bed a long time. The farmer generously took care of the monk. The monk was totally healed because of this care.

"I cannot thank you enough for helping me so much during my lengthy recuperation and for providing me such good care. Since I am a poor traveling monk, I have no material objects to reward you, but instead I will teach you the *kenpô* in which I am trained." Then the monk taught the farmer his method of *kenpô*, and at the time of leaving, he said, "You should never harm people with this *kenpô*. Please use it only when you have to defend yourself."

Several years later, two bandits attacked the farmer's house. "Give us money," they demanded. "I am poor, as you can see from this house. I do not have any money. Please don't harm me."

"You do not have money? Then we are going to make money by selling you into servitude."

Then the bandit tried to twist up the farmer's hand. As if reacting automatically, the farmer's hands and feet struck out. The two bandits fell to the ground, blood coming from their mouths.

From that day on, the farmer lost his docile nature, which he was born with, and went out to do *musha shugyo* while flaunting his ability. Anywhere he went, he won fight after fight and became more arrogant each time. In spite of himself, he started to think that he was the strongest man in the world.

He traveled to Enkyo, where the city was a busy marketplace. He found a young woman who was demonstrating and spoke to people on the streets. "Listen up everyone! Try to hit me or kick me. If your fist touches me, I will give you this money. If my hand hits you first, you lose. I will get your money instead."

Several men challenged her, curious and obsessed with her fiery spirit. The young woman won every time and took their money.

The farmer was watching the matches. He said, "I am next" and made a *kamae* after breaking through the crowd to step forward.

"You should not do this," said the young woman, stepping back.

"Ha, ha... Do you grudge me money or life?!"

The farmer recklessly threw punches at the young woman. At first he thought it would be child's play to defeat her, but after she dodged his punches like a butterfly, his face started to get red with anger, and he began to breathe heavily. Then his vision started to dull, and he felt like he was sinking into the ground legs first. After a while, he found himself watching stars twinkling in front of his eyes.

"Oh, you have come to yourself," another voice spoke, startling him back to reality.

"Aaaa. You are the monk that taught me!"

"Yes. Excuse me; this young woman is named Cho. She is my private student. When she saw your *kamae,* she thought you were a fellow student and asked you to stop. She thought she could not just avoid your strikes and that she might have to harm you... considering she is still a young woman, please forgive her."

"I am deeply ashamed of myself... I never believed that could be such a beautiful and strong woman in the whole world. Learning from this experience, I am only going to use my *kenpô* to protect myself as you told me."

"Where are you going now?"

"I am going back to my native land and become a farmer."

"Is that so? Will you marry this young woman?"

The two were married and lived in peace thereafter.

Since the old days, there have been few warriors that declare themselves senile when they truly are senile. As it happens, Takamatsu *sensei* had the artist name of *Moroku* [play on words for "senility"].

If you try to show off your strength or be arrogant about it and keep training in *budô*, you will fall into being conceited and make a fool out of yourself like Don Quixote [character who was a hilarious fool].

Confucius, a pious man, never showed off or bragged about "*Kairiki Ranshin*" ('*kai*' means strange things of the world; '*riki*' means heroic story; '*ran*' means abnormal deeds; '*shin*' means uncanny power beyond human ability).

Once a novice of *bugei* has succeeded in defeating an opponent with one *waza*, he will instantly be in rapture and consider himself strong. But you should leave him alone until he himself finds that it is only a premature joy. In the world of *budô*, it is very unnatural to think only about strong and weak, because that person will eventually recognize that he is not as strong as he believes.

The weaker and more trivial one is, the sooner he will try to attack an opponent's weak points and defenseless parts. However, a wise person will not attack upon detecting these points, even if you intentionally show him *suki* [unguarded points].

NINJA POPULARITY AND ME

The ninja boom... Somebody threw me into the midst of this media explosion. "I heard some ninja-like young man lives in Noda. It will make an interesting article. Go get some information! It sounds entertaining."

Somebody must have made this statement. They still come to me for research, from everywhere, some half-serious, and some seeming nervous. Each time I have to discuss the same things about ninjutsu as if I was chanting. Yet, when these articles are published, some things are totally misquoted. They even add things I never said.

A foreign journalist who was familiar with Japan and comprehends Japanese writing wanted to introduce this [ninjutsu] to the western culture. Because his blue eyes, like a Siamese cat's, did not have a distorted image about ninjutsu, he accurately described ninjutsu.

For the movie ***Shinobi no mono*** (film adaptation of the book by Murayama Tomoyoshi, director Yamamoto Satsuo, starring Ichikawa Raizo) I was called to go to the movie studio and was asked to teach acting and provide historical research. This movie was a huge hit, becoming a series for the **Daiei** [movie studio] company.

In the **Toho** [movie studio] company animation film ***Kaze no Fujimaru***, the director Shirakawa and a few staff members came to ask me for help.

"After the ***Kaze no Fujimaru*** project, we are planning to make a program called ***Ninjutsu Senichiya***, and we want you to tell the story of ninjutsu."

"What kind of story is the animation of ***Kaze no Fujimaru***?"

"Well, it features ***Kaze no Fujimaru***, who is a boy ninja. We would like to create a humanistic story based on our past ninja comics."

"I agree with your intention. For my part, I want you to make the animation into the Japanese version of **The One Thousand and One Arabian Nights**. I would like to make an animation for children which they can learn something from by watching."

Kaze no Fujimaru consists of 6,000 drawings (for thirty minutes — the usual TV animation uses 4,000 drawings). It is a superb animation with smooth movement.

Then I had a conversation with Ms. Honma Chiyoko [actress] (wife of singer Moriya Hiroshi) in the studio where the television show ***Ninjutsu Senichiya*** is made.

"Hello, *sensei*. What can you tell us tonight?"

She smiles at me theatrically. I did not move my facial muscles freely and said, "Well, shall I talk about *shuriken*?"

I had a hard time trying to change my native dialect Noda dialect into Edo dialect. We spent an hour and a half for only three minutes running time for actual broadcasting. During this taping, we ordered the flower arrangement changed many times because fresh flowers last only twenty minutes. It took us about seven hours to tape a ninjutsu action scene.

For the movie **007**, the principal people behind the project including Albert Broccoli [Producer], Harry Saltzman, Lewis Gilbert [Director], and Ken Adam [art director] visited my small house, questioned me about ninjutsu, and observed my explanations and performance of ninjutsu enthusiastically.

"You are the leader of the ninja. Can you provide us with about two hundred ninja?" Or, "In an open space with no shelter, can some ninja hide and show up with hundreds more?"

I smiled wryly, in spite of myself, at these questions and said, "Since there are only a few ninja in Japan, if you want hundreds you have to gather people like adventure club members, rangers, gymnastics students, carpentry specialists, and lumber jacks."

"For the entrance of great numbers of ninja, we can use a camera trick easily." They went back to the countryside with a promise to meet again. After a while I got a telephone call and they said they would like to meet with me at a distant hotel at 1:00 PM. I arrived at the hotel ten minutes before one. Then the Japanese staff of **007** came and asked me to wait until 6:00 PM because the executives could not come until then.

I have a principle that if I set a time for a meeting with my friends; I will be there and wait for five minutes. These people were trying to make me wait five hours... I lost the willingness to teach them anymore.

The next day, I received so many telephone calls from Mr. Broccoli asking me to come again. I refused. I wanted them to know that not all Japanese have a subservient complex toward foreigners, and that there is a Japanese who has the pride of a warrior. Probably, I am the only one who did not cooperate with **007** upon being asked. When you ride upon a tide, you have to keep your body in balance; otherwise, you will be swallowed by the tide.

TRAINING WILL STILL BE FUN AFTER THE MASTER IS GONE

"You must be lonely since you do not have children, aren't you?" people ask. However, I do not feel lonely at all. I have many children in the martial arts. If there is an individual who wants to succeed me, I think that will be fine. I am very optimistic.

In the age of Okuni Nushi no Mikoto [god], if people found a child superior to their own, they would name him a 'child of god' even though they are not blood related, and make him reign over their province.

I think that was beneficial for both people and society. At times I maintained I had better not have children because my children would be slow and have to practice so hard just to be average.

From the old days, there seem to be very few children who can succeed those people called *kensei* [sword saint]. The concept of inheritance is derived from regret. It is better to think that when people die they go back to the soil, turn into nutrition for the soil, and feed the creatures. To think about life after death is for spiritually immature people. People only live once. However, logical think is often difficult and even Taiko [Toyotomi Hideyoshi] allowed his political enemy to end his reign because he loved his children so much. This may be the same kind of predicament as the scandals regarding medical college entrance exams. [Rich physicians would "procure" for their children passing grades so that their child could take over the family practice.]

Many couples adopt a child because they are distressed by the fact that they cannot have children. Later, this sometimes causes turmoil among their family members. What a pity. It is sometimes better to give away your fortune to those in need or in shelters, and forget the inheritance for the children, rather than let this mess happen. It would make more people happy, would it not?

It is often said that the person who is on top in a hierarchy is lonely, but I never think so. Even martial artists who still have a belief of being lonely should be called naive.

Takamatsu *sensei* used to say, "It would be fun to sit by oneself in a well. And more fun if you could draw pictures in there. I enjoy drawing and hate it when I am bothered while I am painting. Nobody would come if you were in the well, would they? It would be so much fun."

A man who has intense confidence cannot be lonely. Good people like to be around a person with strong confidence, while bad people would stay away. One day, *sensei* told me, "Hatsumi you may not become a *tatsujin* [accomplished person] but you will surely become a *meijin* [distinguished person]."

"Thank you. I will be content if I can become a *meijin*." However, I was rather discouraged when I thought I could not become a *tatsujin*. Now I think martial artists should make an effort not to be ashamed to be an expert of *budô* for their whole life. A *tatsujin* means to become a complete human being. In order to do so, the first thing a person must learn is to endure. One must think compassionately toward others. Doing so, the person would be respected as a great man. Like those people who became famous by doing good deeds, these are *meijin*. Therefore, to become a *meijin* you must learn *mushin* [no-mind].

IF YOU DO NOT HAVE ANYTHING, USE THE SHINOBI TOOL

When I was asked to supervise the play called ***Sengoku Meimei Den*** [Legend in the Era of Battle] at the famous Teigeki theater, I took eight students with me. We performed a combat demonstration that was almost real before the audience; the audience consisted of actors and staff members. Some of the attendees were Hanato Kobako [writer], Frankie Sakai [actor], Nagato Isamu [actor], Nakamura Katsuo [actor], Baisho Mitsuko [actress] and Yasuda Michiyo [actress]. In the outline issued for this play, it was written "What a surprise! *Togakure ryu ninpô* practitioners astounded the cast with fierce *kihaku* [inner power] when they performed an almost real demonstration."

I graciously turned down the offer from the Teigeki staff to act in the play for a month. The reason was that I found it to be like a Moriel burlesque or satire when I read the script.

There are six tools of the ninja, which consist of *amigasa, kaginawa, ishifude, kusuri, sanjaku tenugui,* and *uchitake. Amigasa* is used to hide the face and to hide secret messages. *Kaginawa* is a hook used to catch upon tree branches, or a tall fence, and climb over to escape. It was also used like *kusarigama* to take a sword away or to catch onto running horses or humans, and drag them down. *Ishifude* is a small granite stone, used to write secret codes on a pillar, a fence, or a wall. *Kusuri* [medicine] is for emergency treatment. The ninja carried a restorative medicine for cuts and sometimes carried poisons. *Uchitake* is like a hand warmer, a bamboo container that holds fire; it is used for *katon no jutsu* [fire escape methods]. *Sanjaku tenugui* [three feet long head wrap] is dyed midnight blue and conceals in the darkness. It can also be used as a filter to purify dirty water for drinking. One could even wrap a stone with it and make a weapon called *fundo tenugui. Sanjaku tenugui* was also sometimes used as a bandage.

Although these are called the six tools, there are tens of ways to use them, not only six ways. Moreover, depending upon the tradition, the six tools may be different. So, if I am asked how many ninja tools there are, I can only answer that there are innumerable tools. The number of *ryuha* [traditions] also varies — seventy *ryu,* seventy-three *ryu,* and seventy-five *ryu.* Each *ryuha* has a tool according to its *tongyo.*

There is a way to feign as if you have a tool, when actually you do not have any. It is called *nakute aru dogu* [tool that does not exist]. This is the ultimate tool for ninja, and only the smartest ninja can use it.

In this age that is not lacking in materials, I hope there are more ninja who can use this last tool without losing hope and admitting defeat. If you can only use certain kinds of tools [or weapons] that you prefer or that pertain to you, you are not a fully competent ninja. The person who can use one tool in many ways can be called a real ninja.

DO NOT DEPEND ON ESP

The prophecies of Nostrodamus have become best-selling books. Recently, people seem to believe that those with ESP are superior beings. If people try to develop ESP and then succeed, and then they rely on it, I am afraid their original human senses may become weaker.

Yuri Geller [famous psychic] was very popular in Japan for his reported strong ESP. He supposedly could bend a fork using mental power, read minds, see future events, and was clairvoyant. However, when he went to a Las Vegas casino, his clairvoyant power and his willpower did not work at all, and he lost miserably. ESP is like an animal's special sense if you interpret it primitively. Thus, it can be said that Yuri Geller's losses in Las Vegas were because of his human senses.

Martial artists should not rely solely upon ESP. For a certain period, I train my students to appreciate and acquire ESP. After this period is over, I teach them the importance of refining their human senses. Once you are caught up in developing metal powers, you may go down a blind path all your life, led by some ridiculous sect or fortuneteller.

GYOKKO RYU TEN RYAKU UCHU GASSHO

Although this is not only the case in the modern times, both religious leaders and their followers seem to measure the merit of things only by their monetary value. They pray to God for profit and protection — these actions make them totally possessed — more than mere egotists do. I think that nothing is wrong with uniqueness. It is even okay to base a religion upon this. The important thing is to know the theology's direction after you have entered the training of that particular religion.

Politely speaking, a person should continue to do virtuous deeds, leaving his ego behind, and then discover the joy of identifying with the universe and gain a feeling of awareness. This is the first step to understanding the universe. Then people will understand the morals of how they should live.

This is the same for *budô*. As with the limitations of winning or losing, how can you understand *budô* only by thinking of give and take? I tell my students, "Drop your desire." As in the essence of *budô*, I wish them to perceive physical harmony by surrendering their personal victory.

Martial arts must have a perspective of the nature, which transcends the expectation of winning and losing. The only way to this understand this is to study the virtue of *budô*. Then gain [*toku*] may turn into virtue [*toku*] and begin to turn a warrior [*bujin*] to martial virtue [*bujin*].

Therefore, *tenryaku uchu gassho* means to start training after making *gassho* [palms clasped in front of you] with *jin* devotion, *gi* loyalty, *rei* manners, *chi* wisdom, *shin* faith, *chi* earth, *sui* water, *ka* fire, *fu* wind, and *ku* void.

LIVE ON A RATIO OF 7:3

If it were true that the older you get, the younger you want to be, it would also be true that older people fade away first.

There are two kinds of human desire. One is to make oneself flourish and the other is to self-destruct. While people repeat these things, they begin saying ideas like, "Life is not fully lived until you die; yet there is life after death." To simplify this idea, we can say they start to reason life and death. Clearly, they lack the self-restraint.

When a person finds something more important than making a living, he will chase that and forget about making a living. Otherwise, he feels cannot attain it. While you are eating, you will never catch a parting object. Therefore, when you decide to attain something important, speed swiftly upon that path.

Katsu Kaishu threw everything away, because he thought studying Dutch with a book was more important than living life. It must have been a drastic situation; not simply that he just threw away his life, but everybody has a period in which he can concentrate on only one thing. When that time comes, you had better walk straight on the path ahead.

If a person only thinks about eating, he will weaken both his brain and his body. Again, to live life on the 7:3 ratio is important. By continuing this attitude toward life — this must be the secret way to become perceptive.

WHEN MUDDY WATER TURNS TO CLEAR WATER

Sometimes you can enter smoothly from the back of the house, when it is hard to get in the front door. It is very wrong to approach everything in a straightforward fashion. Although I have been deceived many times, I think the accumulation of experience is like the collecting of volatile substances that eventually burst into flames.

There are people who quit when they find out they have been cheated but those people never will be noble people. I used a devious, roundabout way of *shugyo* until I grasped the real *budô*. Now, looking back, those experiences were not wasted time. I now can see that each one was a step. I find value even in deviousness.

If you stay calm in muddy water, you will understand that the mud sinks to the bottom and the water becomes clear. This is *injutsu*.

I heard that Takamatsu *sensei*'s teacher Toda Shinryuken *sensei* quit the headmaster position of a *budô* school when Lord Ii, Chief Minister of the Shogun, was inaugurated and traveled around the Kinki District. The *denshô* does not state the reason he quit his position but I believe I understand. He probably thought fighting would break out and that it made no sense for Japanese people to fight against each other.

Budô for dissension is a misuse of lessons. Apparently, he wanted to teach this fact. Therefore, he did not run away from the current of his times. He must have done that because he understood his community.

DECEPTIVENESS AND TRUTH OF STARING INTO THE ENEMY

On occasion, I speak about my teacher, about his virtue and quality. However, sometimes my students show respect for my teacher and forget about my existence. While I was unable to grasp the fact that *sôke* is between teacher and students, I scolded myself about living in this middle space, but the moment I found myself there I understood the secret of *ikkan fuyu* [unconscious movement].

My wife has been practicing *Odori* [Japanese dance] for fifteen years. One day when I asked her, "When you watch Japanese dancing, where do you look?"

She said, "Well, I see the eyes of the dancer. Of course, the style and the rhythm are important, but their eyes are the deciding factor of whether the dancing is alive or dead."

In *budô*, we also place importance on the eyes' expression. Whenever I see the acting with eyes by Mr. Shimomoto Tsutomu in ***Kita no Kazoku*** [Northern Family], and think of the attractiveness of Mr. Hasegawa Kazuo's eyes, I come to realize the importance of acting with the eyes. Especially when there is no dialogue in the scene, it can enliven the acting or render it sterile.

In *budô*, also, when there is no *kiai* or other sound, the power of the eyes (the illusiveness or veracity of *metsuke* [fixing the gaze]) often decides who will win and lose.

Metsuke is just like adding flavor to the cuisine; it is indispensable to make art come alive.

CREATION FROM MADNESS

I used to be scolded by my grandfather; "You talk boastfully. But what is so good about that? We call children like you egotistic."

Put my own case aside. Those who are megalomaniacs, those who have timid and fearful hearts, those who have persecution mania, and those who have schizophrenia can often be a source of new ideas. The person who does not have a mind that wanders into madness will not have great vitality or creativity. From madness, *shingan* [god's eye] will be born — the creative power.

One day someone discussed the suicides of Mr. Kawabata Yasunari and Mr. Mishima Yukio. "Why did those people die, when they had status, fame and fortune? They did not seem to have any dissatisfaction ... Or, maybe they were people who were too smart to live on the edge of madness."

I answered, "There might be some people who think a madman is a deviant. The people who are called 'common men' live a life in a typical mold, which is really an uncommon way of living. And also, they usually have little awareness of themselves."

The writing style of Mr. Hanato Kobako, who is called "bullet train author," is fragmented. Mr. Hanato has a room with a counter in his house, and he puts manuscripts in three places on the counter. Once he gets tired of working on one piece, he starts to work on the next one. In this fashion, he can complete three different stories well without confusion. He must be unusually talented.

DIG THE GRAVE DEEP AND WIDE

It is said that both elephants and cats instinctively realize the time of their death before they die. Among all creatures, there is no one more miserable than humans, that do not know their time of death. And the majority of people today belong in this category. They do not know their time of death and are going to die after living blindly. Without knowing the true nature of death, they are going to die of their fear of death.

The elephant that is going to sleep under the white moon or the cat who is trying to sleep slowly after hiding himself... therein exists an unwritten law of nature. We humans also should have room to think and plan for the next life before we go down into the earth to sleep. The people who do not have a readiness for death will float in the world of perverse dream after their death without knowing they are dead.

The people who cannot sleep in a "limitless" grave cannot go to heaven. They must be floating in the universe because of the shortage of grave sites, just like the shortage of houses. Maybe, it is because of this that people today are trying to go to heaven by listening to the chanting of Buddhist scripture while they are still alive. This is more miserable than laughable.

A graveyard is the place to praise the people who have lived their lives. I would like to dig my grave deep and wide and place ornaments around it. The *kofun* [ancient burial mound] must have been completed in the times when such feeling was still alive and well.

CUT OFF YOUR FEELINGS

Every time people from the intelligentsia are caught in a scandal, the public says scornful things to them as if to compare themselves to those individuals. An intellectual is an artisan of the mind. People respect artisans because of their spirit.

Among martial art practitioners, there are many regarded as artisans of *bujutsu*. Therein is begotten the spirit of *bujin*. Only these people get respect as masters of *budô* and are called true martial artists. A person who lacks this spirit will not make it as a martial artist or as anything else.

Returning to the former story, the most astonishing and annoying thing about scandals among intelligentsia is that the people in this class defend each other based on friendship and teacher-student relationship.

If you are influenced by feelings, you will lose your way. Is it because the cord of emotion is covered with sticky adhesive and attached by spiritual ichor? The cord of emotion tends to stick to unhealthy relationships easily.

It can only be said that a weak spirit becomes bound with strange friendships or strange love and is unable to sever these ties when necessary. I believe that as a human being and because of the obligations of *budô* it is a natural thing to sever these emotions.

In the connection of teachers and students, friendship and love relationships — if you cannot sever these feelings, you should deem that you are being cut. This is possible for a person who studied the martial arts to do this because he knows how to cut [with a sword].

However, an uncultivated person is bound by these emotional ties and will unknowingly end up with his head cut off. You must have inner strength and courage to sever this distorted sentimentality.

NEWTON AND THE APPLE

It is said that Newton realized the earth had gravity when he saw an apple fall to the ground. Thereafter he enunciated, "Principia." If I am allowed to translate this in my own way, gravity is a power to protect the earth or the universe. William Tell shot an arrow through an apple resting on his son's head. Nasuno Yoichi [famous legend] shot down the fan of Heike with an arrow. Did these individuals know about the law of gravity or not...

If you believe there is a power that pulls things toward each other in the universe, it could be taken for granted that you can hit the mark with a straight mind. If you translate this fact in Buddhism, it would be a thought of *innen* [cause and effect] or *rinne* [the circle of life]. My teacher made up the organization called *Shinshinkai* [sincere minded assembly].

I translate Newton's law of gravity to mean the power to eliminate the unnatural, with harmony between the law of gravity and *bushin* [martial spirit]. There is a level called *shizen shigoku* [essence through nature] in the mastery of my *budô*. This is it. First, you should know gravity is the power to protect. In addition, water's buoyancy helps when you fight in the rivers. It is the harmony of nature in the essence of *bugei*, too.

BOYS BE PROUD

When I taught a child who was labeled a "failure," I noticed, repeatedly, he was no different than an average child. Since I had that experience, I started to teach children in my *dojo*, also.

All children are different; they have their own characteristics. Firstly, my objective is to draw out their individual qualities and to give them the self-confidence to be themselves. Then, the individual attributes start to shine as the boys' special art. Once a person has a special art or skill, he can have an objective and confidence in life.

Compared to a child, it is much harder to discover the special gifts of young adults. If a person starts searching through religion or ideology and deviates from it, he gets into blind faith or unbalanced love, then he is consumed by his own ideas and by the people around him and destroys everything. You have to make an effort to put out such a "blaze" as soon as you find it. Therefore, there are five rules in my *dojo*.

1. ***You must know the perseverance to last an unknown period of time.***

2. ***You must know mankind's path is justice.***

3. ***You must forget the mind of greed, pleasure, and corruption.***

4. ***You must acquire enlightenment of fudôshin [immovable spirit], regarding grief and regret as nature's law.***

5. ***You must never forget the path of dedication and you must study literature and budô extensively and sincerely.***

You must keep these five rules in mind.

Let me explain *chuko* [loyalty] because young people today tend to claim this word is feudalistic. "*Chu*" means respect and keeping harmony among people. "*Ko*" means to give, to devote, and to forget oneself.

These five rules were set by Toda Shinryuken *sensei* but there are a considerable number of students dedicated to training who violate these rules. Only a person who can lead these students has the qualifications and value as a *shihan* [master instructor]. You have to strictly prohibit conversation during practice about subjects such as politics, religion, money, women, and gambling, because these things cause you to diminish your adamant study of *budô*. If people exchange such conversations during practice, you had better direct them toward reasserting to *budô*.

A CERTIFICATE OF DEATH

When I give my students the writing of *menkyo kaiden*, I declare to them, "Take this *menkyo kaiden* as a certificate of death. You are dead from today on." In this case, death means to nullify one's self. The 'self' means earthly desires. In other words, you should become *hotoke* [Buddha] and heavenly.

A person who cannot eliminate earthly desires even after he receives *menkyo kaiden* can never cut his own body. Such a person is better off abandoning being a warrior and living honestly as an animal. After all, an animal is only an animal. In olden times, a Samurai used to inscribe *hisetsu.* This means to inhumanely cut off earthly desires.

Spiritual power cuts earthly desire like one swing of a sword. As stated in the document of *ittoryodan* [cut in half with a downswing], "There is a method to cut good from bad, to separate these two. This method is the essence of the way of the sword."

The one who has received the "certificate of death" must live for others and for society. It is natural for a *bujin* to instantly expel a person who cannot assume this obligation.

READ A BOOK AS IF YOU ARE CONVERSING WITH IT

There is the opinion that it is not so useful to read a book when you become an adult. That is because books no longer have a strong impact upon an adult and adults' memories weaken over the years. They cannot discern and appreciate good sentences or good phrases. That may be true but I do not agree with it. I have never let a book, no matter how famous the author, influence me. I think it is better to approach a book by trying to "consider" it after you have established your own opinion. That means you can only truly read a book when you grow up, doesn't it?

Of course, I would not deny the view of any reader who tries to find a world he does not know through books. Yet, to read a book and gain knowledge, and then to become blind to other ways of learning about the world, becomes a problem. It contains danger. Therefore, if you can compare the world of books and the world that you actually know, and try to read the book as if you were having a discussion with it, I think that would be an ideal reading method.

Some books contain erroneous details, including weekly magazines, because books are written with writers' emotions and thoughts as the foundation. If the expression of inaccuracy is too great, it is because the writer's point of view is exaggerated. Therefore, some people who do not know society well might accept the exaggerations and believe them to be real.

There are methods to find out the difference between knowledge acquired through books and practical learning. However, we have to think about how difficult it is for a person to see reality once he becomes too influenced by a book. When you grow old, you increasingly tend to prefer easy-reading magazines. That is all right. But I would like to advise people who think that they are too old to read serious writings at their age that, "Now is the time to read serious writing and have a conversation with a book."

DO NOT FORGET YAMATO DAMASHII

I always tell my friends who travel abroad, "Have *Yamato Damashii* where ever you travel." Some people frown when I say this, telling me that they feel a martial artist's mind is filled with thoughts of aggression and fighting. There seems to be a vast difference in meaning of *Yamato Damashii* from the viewpoint of the general public and martial artists. Since I wish you all bear this *Yamato Damashii* when you travel, I will explain what I mean and cast aside all misunderstandings.

As they say, during the war this phrase certainly contained a unique connotation in regarding battle. There was a frightful attitude that you could win a personal victory through *Yamato Damashii* even if the battle was lost. That is why many of the people who were in such battles reject the phrase *Yamato Damashii.*

However, I think the phrase "*Yamato Damashii*" is an admirable phrase. It offers the Japanese quality of life. *Yamato Damashii* literally means "Japanese spirit" and puts strong emphasis upon harmony. This is the martial artist's true *Yamato Damashii.*

Budô is never meant to be a weapon for aggression. There are times when it is necessary to use *budô* for such purposes, but at least the fundamental mind of martial artists are not for fighting. The real purpose of a martial artist is to shake hands with many people. Therefore, a martial artist's basic frame of mind should be nothing but *Yamato Damashii.*

The reason I say, "Have *Yamato Damashii* where ever you travel," is for the purpose of becoming friends with people abroad with utmost forbearance, and let them know the true heart of the Japanese.

For the above reasons, the true master of *budô* avoids fighting until all other possibilities have been tried. By avoiding a confrontation, one finds the smartest way to become friends with an opponent.

It is very immature to pick a fight in hope of showing off your technique when you have only trained in *budô* for a very short time. Likewise, pretending to know everything and showing off your knowledge does not make people feel comfortable. If you wish to truly understand *Yamato Damashii*, you must learn these matters well.

MUSASHI'S COUNTERPUNCH

A famous boxer can throw a skillful counterpunch. His punches alone are not too strong, but he uses strategy to knock down his opponent. This methodology resembles the theory of *budô*, "When you are protecting a castle a single soldier has the power to defend against three times as many enemy soldiers." This was also one of Miyamoto Musashi's principles. This technique is one that people should be encouraged to use.

Musashi had a duel on Ganryujima Island. He upset his opponent, Kojiro, after he had made him wait for a long time and then, finally arrived late for the fight. Once there he said, "Kojiro, you lost." This was the crux of his counterattack.

But if I only emphasize this part of the story, that may annoy many people because they may think Musashi acted cowardly to avoid a fair fight and anxiously applied psychological control over Kojiro. However, if this all had been carefully planned in advance by Musashi and he had even prepared *waza* [technique] according to his scheme, we should pay him respect anyway, shouldn't we?

During his training period, Musashi acquired the essence of counter-attack when he saw wild cats making defensive postures against a hawk. Then he began practicing *ukemi* by repeatedly landing upon his feet after tumbling down from a height like a cat. Following this, he practiced how to overcome an opponent after being thrown by that person. Then Musashi practiced a complex punch, which was launched at the opponent's suki, the instant the opponent threw him. Ultimately, he made this technique the essence of *Musashi ryu taijutsu*.

He not only aggravated Kojiro but he calculated the application of his *Musashi ryu taijutsu* counterpunch, most effectively. There is so much criticism directed at Musashi regarding his not belonging to the assembly of famous sword masters, but the reason he never lost any confrontation might be attributable to this counterpunch.

Even today, power alone cannot win a fight. Sometimes, you have to face an opponent with superior strength. Even then, there is a way to win.

My suggestion is that we learn from this "Musashi counterattack." Openly appear to yield to the opponent. Then you will notice a *suki* in the opponent *kamae*. This is when you should attack. While you look at various opponents from a distance and see their apparently greater power, if you keep sighing, you do not have any chance.

If you have time to sigh, you should have enough time to devise a way to find the opponent's *suki*. Musashi only agreed to fight with Kojiro after Kojiro had confronted him two previous times; therefore, Musashi actually "sighed" twice before the final confrontation.

LONG LIVE JAPANESE TRADITION

Years ago, my students and I did a *Togakure ryu ninpô happo hiken* demonstration at the martial arts convention sponsored by the Nippon Kachu Kenkyukai [club that studies armor]. As we were about to begin, the chairperson asked, "Is everything ready?"

"We are ready," I answered for my students and myself. We stepped toward the stage. Halfway down the hall, one teacher came from the further end and said, "You must cancel the demonstration. Everyone is drinking *sake* in the main hall." I casually bowed to the man and continued toward the stage. There seemed to be some trouble among the sponsors but I was in an immovable state of mind [*fudôshin*]. The curtain went up and our performance began. As I looked at the audience, there were many distinguished *sensei* and beautiful *geisha*, too. I smelled *sake*.

We all bowed and began the *taijutsu* demonstration as I stood at the center of my students. The audience became quiet, almost totally silent, due to fierceness of our performance. Many had even forgotten the drinks in their hands. However, one member of the audience began pouring *sake* into a cup, trying to prepare a drink. I waited until he brought the cup to his mouth and then let forth a loud *kiai*. The sound of my "EI!" as I moved through the demonstration, caused him to drop the cup from his hand.

We continued through all our presentations and then retired backstage when we were finished. Many instructors came to speak with us and gave us encouraging support, saying "*gokurousama*" [I appreciate your efforts]. One person asked me how I thought the event had gone.

I explained that the demonstration had shown my philosophy of *nin* [perseverance]. We continued our talk on the way home. I asked the man what he had noticed. "Surely, you grasped the importance of *kihaku* [inner power] through today's demonstration? Did you notice how we never showed discouragement or defeat, no matter how unfortunate the circumstances? If you have faith in your heart and are virtuous, strength fills you. I believe that almost everyone at the hall watched our performance until its end, without a drink. It seemed that some of the older men, who had been overdrinking, were quite attentive and alert toward the end. Maybe, we even put too much power into it."

My devoted students seem to understand that a person's strength does not lie solely in his muscles but in the spirit. My students all looked confident and happy.

Weeks later, we did a demonstration and gave a speech at the society for foreign representatives. After initial greetings from the NBC News Chairman of the Far East Branch and German press representative, we showed a *ninpô* movie that had been broadcast on NTV. I narrated it. Then, we presented a color dramatization of *ninpô* originally shot with 16-mm film. The film had been made to publicize *ninpô* to the world. In this film, we included *kunoichi no jutsu* because I have heard that many television viewers enjoyed watching a woman defeat a male attacker.

After the film presentations, we presented a lecture and a live demonstration about *taijutsu*, *sojutsu*, *kenjutsu*, and mysterious training such as — *moku, ka, do, kin,* and *sui no jutsu...* The foreigners seemed to watch without blinking their eyes.

Several days later, two buses brought several foreign newspaper writers to visit my dojo. During those demonstrations, I played background music in order to fill the breaks and enhance the overall effect of the show.

Takamatsu *sensei* told me that if you use a sword in a demonstration, you should do a *kenbu* [martial sword dance]. For this reason, I have studied Shimai and Noh, along with Japanese dancing and acting. I believe that we should learn the balance and rhythm between training, acting, and playing music by learning these arts.

I feel strongly about learning both hard and soft martial arts. Henceforth, we should plan demonstrations that blend hard and soft movements. Furthermore, we should remember to delight people all over the world by putting dramatic elements in our demonstrations.

Mizutani Yaeko [famous actress] voiced similar statements on the day she received a cultural merit award. "I have been acting since I was six years old... Now, that is almost sixty years. These days I think about how to please the audience rather than contemplating about myself as an artist. I was only acting as a craftsperson. I never thought I could be elected as a cultural contributor..."

In Ms. Mizutani's speech, she made a statement regarding her "acting as a craftsperson" which represents a beautiful attitude toward acting. Only a person that lives with this attitude could know this state of mind. We Japanese do not feel self-consciousness about using the word "craftsperson" as opposed to "artist." I feel that this offers praise to both artists and craftspeople.

We should arrange theatrical presentations and displays with a modern ambience based upon the ancient genius of craftsmanship and the depth of skill associated with it. If we neglect to do so, the Japanese traditional arts will die out. Yukio Mishima once said this to me:

"Please cherish the beauty and grandeur of the Japanese traditions. People who master these traditions are becoming rare and vanishing. There is only one person in all of Japan, probably only one person in the whole world that can master the Japanese cultural treasure of *ninpô budô*. Mr. Hatsumi, please keep it well and treasure it."

WRITE WITH A CANDID BUT INOFFENSIVE STYLE

At the beginning of this book, the President of the publishing company asked me, "Please be candid." However, since a book remains forever, and it is not the Samurai way to provoke readers by mischievousness, I have tried to write with a candid but inoffensive style.

My reason for doing this is to express my own assertions without offending my readers and public. I would like people who work for today's mass communication industry to read this: Please, be careful not to hurt anyone when you write using an aggressive method.

I do not believe it is right to simply sell many books or to get high television ratings. If that is the only important thing for these individuals, they are not much different from malicious agitators. Today, the issue of "freedom of speech" or "silencing the press" is openly and loudly debated. Is there such a tendency on the rise? It is very important to use a pointed but inoffensive method [of writing] to make people reflect upon themselves without offending them. You should encourage them. How can you be an adult, be a guiding influence, and encourage people by shouting and acting like mischievous children?

There was a popular saying among children for a while: "All adults are bad." This must be attributed to adults' irresponsible criticisms. When you hear children's astute irony, we adults need to reflect upon ourselves honestly before saying, "Kids today are..." Conscientious *budôka* would only reprimand people or things when they assessed it acceptable to do so. They also raised and lowered their tones accordingly.

CONTEMPORARY LITERATURE AS SEEN BY MARTIAL ARTISTS

Every writer has his or her own style of writing. Writing styles change according to the period in which a writer lives. It should change according to their environment, too. These days, the *fude* [Japanese calligraphy brush] has changed into a pen, and printing, typing, and audiotapes have been made into moving pictures. The expression of our written characters is changing away from handwriting because of TV, photographs, and movies. In addition, Japanese literature writers will inevitably move away from using *kanji.*

Discussing serious literature — sometimes a story becomes more interesting when you listen to it rather than read it. That is because the narrator, the so-called *kataribe* [historians or storytellers of ancient days] makes the hard-to-read sentences rhythmic, and we find that delightfully humorous.

With a good storyteller, or "body language announcer," if you hand these people pens, they might come up with quasi-literature. In order to enter the world of true literature, I suggest they become experienced in a variety of adventures, be contemplative, and finally, become a person with strong creativity.

A pen (or brush) is an extension of the fingers. In ancient times, our fingers represented *chi, sui, ka, fu, ku, moku, ka, do, kin, sui, jin, gi, rei, chi, shin,* etc... Among martial artists, those who could read and write well were influenced by poetry and wrote "songs of mastery"; the concepts or lessons they did not express clearly have been left as mysterious verses. Things they could not express in writing they added by *kuden* [oral teachings].

But anyway, I think when these individuals were busy practicing training they must have held weapons and did not have much time to spend holding a pen or brush. There may have been a few warriors who were able to afford some time to write autobiographical *denshô* [written transmissions]. It is a shame that while most of the *bugei ryuha* evolved around the end of Muromachi period [1333 - 1573] we have *denshô* mostly from the Edo period [1603 - 1867].

Samurai had the habit of leaving a death poem and sending his opponent a poem before their battle. I wonder if some of these were recorded in the *denshô* full of verses as a part of their tradition.

Anyway, the expression of a martial artist's writings is derived from his movements and memories. These writings are an art form used to communicate the actions of combat, a *kata,* experience, history, etc. I believe that some of our modern literary techniques began these ideas. There is a tendency for martial philosophy to affect all of one's writings.

LISTEN TO EXPERIENCE!

The word "experience" seems to remind weekly magazine gossip columnists about their first intimate relations. It seems that our young people now only appreciate stories of sincere experience if they are about such intimate relationships. In contrast, when I was little, we used to listen excitedly to the story of Kanto Province's big earthquake or the fires caused by it... stories of common incidents and the necessary knowledge to live life. Our parents shared all this with us. I was always happy to listen to these old stories.

One day, when I analyzed why the famous detective Sherlock Holmes could solve mysteries one after another I came to understand his "knack." I found that the reason he excelled over police detectives was that he knew criminal history, and he listened closely to peoples' explanations. He also said, "Crime repeats, just like history."

In order to survive, you may have to win a battle — in order to keep peace; it is also important to know the history of past experiences.

The world has changed with the arrival of firearms. There are many tales of experience and reason. Fables tell stories of men that attempt to pierce rocks with arrows using their spiritual powers. There are tales and adventures about long-distance archery. Tales of firing more than three thousand arrows. These tales are about endurance and training. We should not overlook any stories of experience, because every challenging experience has some rationality, spiritual power, and fierce training, which is necessary to learn *heihô* [combat strategy].

Contemporary police arrest techniques, which employ combat skills, often lack rationality, and do not reflect the practices of the old days. That is because there are no elders who can tell the true stories of experience. Perhaps there are, but so few instructors listen to these true stories of experience from their seniors. A good story of experience makes you feel more satisfied than when you find a diamond in a mine.

As a senior, if you believe it advantageous to bestow your tale upon a beginner, you should enthusiastically share your past experiences. If I put it in *budô* terms, you should speak about the times when you lost a fight. The story of a lost confrontation is a very important *buyuden* [heroic story] to show that these mistakes should not be repeated.

Any person who can tell such stories would be called a man of true courage. Life is full of mistakes. When you make a mistake, you should not wince about it, but you should make it into fertilizer for the future growth of our younger students.

DO NOT STOP EXCESSIVE AMBITION

There seem to be many parents who think, "We would be happy if our child has an average life after he gets a job in a first-rate company." If their child comes to them for advice stating, "I am thinking of leaving my company," most of the parents say, "That is out of the question, no way," without asking the reason. I am opposed to this mentality.

Should our youth not have ambition to rise higher? Some of them fail an entrance exam for college and spend their entire time studying for the following year's test, others fail to enter a company and live searching for other jobs, or some even leave good companies to consider about their personal significance.

Many people who fail an entrance exam or fail to acquire a desired job often have their hearts filled with loneliness. They find themselves feeling insignificant. They are usually afraid and think, "Could this be the end of my dreams? Could this really be the end?" If their parents told them, "The only important thing is to pass the entrance exam," or "Getting a good job is the only thing that matters," this person would feel even more dejected. Parents should advise their children beneficially; help make their lives hopeful. If parents encouraged their children, putting less stress on them, their children would be able to unleash their inspiration to the limit.

Moreover, a person must have good reason and a clear purpose if he wants to leave his first-class job. It is absurdity for parents to get angry without listening to their child at all.

Many martial artists also go through a "drifting period." There are many of these individuals that eventually went on to acquire mastery after this period of feeling restlessness and unattached.

There are other reasons for this behavior, but I believe that it is good to see today's young people turning into a wanderer like *Tora-san*. It would be easy to hinder their ambitions but instead I would like to give them a nudge to help them onward.

To hinder his ambitious nature, I begin by telling him a story to make him worry about his future. His doubt would increase by listening to such a story, and he would lose the nerve to live "on the edge" in the future. Second, you could tell him to have courage. Third, you could make him move out and live alone. Then, when he comes back, sorrowful, you can tell him the reason you gave him the three techniques of "encouragement." In truth, any story you tell is useless until you first let your child find that his desires are unreasonable.

When you leave his fate to the winds or to heaven, there is a tendency for people to become desperate and confront reality. This person needs a push and he needs to look at himself when he gets listless. When I watch TV, I sometimes see chaos that seems incomprehensible but is intentional. The turning point is when you can tell what his next action will be; this may be the key to understanding the necessity of chaos.